praise for Lisa Hammond and *Dream Big*

"Lisa Hammond tells the truth about the challenges of being a female CEO with integrity and heart in this conversational and enticing book. Her candor and authenticity are compelling. I stayed up all night to finish this story of Lisa's adventures, relentless courage, and passion for inspiring and nurturing her customers! This book is a winner."

> — GAIL MCMEEKIN, LICSW, author of
> *The 12 Secrets of Highly Creative Women* and
> *The Power of Positive Choices*

"Lisa Hammond pays homage to the sacred messiness of surrendering to her dream, trusting beginner's mind, and balancing life, love, and sanity in the midst of it all. Lisa shares with us the gifts and challenges of dreaming BIG. Along the way, our own dreams, and our courage, awaken!"

> — PATRICIA LYNN REILLY, author of
> *Imagine a Woman in Love with Herself* and *I Promise Myself*

dream

Finding the Courage
to **Follow Your Dreams**
and Laugh at Your Nightmares

big

Lisa Hammond

The Barefoot CEO
and founder of Femail Creations

CONARI PRESS

First published in 2004 by Conari Press,
an imprint of Red Wheel/Weiser, LLC
York Beach, ME

With offices at:
368 Congress Street
Boston, MA 02210
www.redwheelweiser.com

Book design by Maxine Ressler

LIBRARY OF CONGRESS CATALOGING-IN-PUBLICATION DATA
Hammond, Lisa.
  Finding the courage to follow your dreams and laugh at your
nightmares / Lisa Hammond.
     p. cm.
  ISBN 1-57324-955-6
  1. Women—Psychology. 2. Women—Conduct of life.
3. Self-actualization (Psychology) I. Title.
HQ1206.H236 2004
305.4—dc22   2003024110

Printed in Canada
TCP

11   10   09   08   07   06   05   04
   8   7   6   5   4   3   2   1

I dedicate this book to Jeff, Harlie, and Bridger.

*Without their love and support my own
dream would have been a lot smaller.*

Dream Big

♡

Lisa

contents

DrEAM BiG

MOST DrEAMS GET STAlled, or STOPped, or LOST DVE to <u>FEAr of STArting AT All</u>.

THiS BOOK illvsTrATes THe Deep VAlve if STArting, over and over AGAin. Living one's DrEAM is ABovt Continvally STArting, even WHen All "reAsonABle evidence" Points To THe opposite.

"never, never, never vnder any CircvMSTances, FACe FACTS"

— RvTH Gordon

I love How LiSA HAMMond not only didn't FACe FACTS, Bvt MADe vp new FACTS BASed on new inforMATion SHe received.

PrEAMS need SHeLters, Mentors, and clEAr Pirections ABovt "How to po it," and even More iMPortantly, THey need STories ABovt "How I did it."

<u>DrEAM BiG</u> tells vs in MArvelovs DetAiL How LiSA and Her company,

FeMAiL CreAtions, did it anD Are
Still Doing THeir DreAM. THese stories
anD eXAMples are Full of FresH reasons
WHy you Can Also Do your DreAM!

Lisa points out THAT Vision anD HeART
Are More important THan Financing anD
Business plans. SHe Also DescriBes How
you Can reAlly be yourself anD create
A FulFilling, successful Business anD
DreAM.

THis is not an ideALIZed Account of
How GreAT Her DreAM is, But an unFOLDing
STory of GrowTH, THe necessity of
MisTAKes, anD How Funny nightMares
Can Be WHen viewed in THe LIGHT of
one's DreAM.

SARK (Susan Ariel RAinBow Kennedy) is
THe Founder of CAMP SARK, A company THAT
inspires anD supports creative living THrough
innovative products anD Services. SHe is Also
THe AuTHor anD ARTist of 12 Books, incluDing
THe newesT: MAKe your creative DreAMs ReAL.
visiT SARK AT WWW. CAMPSARK.com

acknowledgments

To my muse and incredible husband, Jeff, for his steadfast support of all of my dreams. For holding down the fort while I followed my passion. For driving me hundreds of miles, so I could spend time in the seclusion of a hotel to unleash my creative juices. For knowing when I needed to be alone and when I needed him there. I will be eternally grateful for his willingness to sustain me in every way.

To my children, who always believe their mom can do anything she puts her mind to. For understanding that the creative process can be chaotic and sleep deprivation can make you cranky. For reminding me what matters and what doesn't. For teaching me far more than I will ever teach you.

To my sisters, who responded to countless emails and spent hours on the phone with me as sounding boards throughout the process of writing this book.

To the wonderful women of Conari Press for their talent and vision. For giving me the nudge I needed to take yet another step outside of my comfort zone and write this book. For their continual support and guidance. For knowing that when women follow their dreams and share their stories, magic can happen!

permission
to dream

*And the day came when the risk it took to
remain tight inside the bud was more painful
than the risk it took to blossom.*

— ANAIS NIN

E VER SINCE I STARTED FEMAIL CREATIONS BACK
in 1996, I have been asked almost daily why I did it.
Sometimes I answer, "a moment of insanity" because, knowing what I know now, I realize I must have been insane to
think I could start a catalog company from the ground
up. Sometimes I say I did it because *I* wanted to shop at a
catalog just like this one, and when it didn't arrive in my
mailbox, I decided to start it myself. Although both of
those answers are based in fact, they don't really get to
the heart of the matter. The truest answer is that I started
Femail Creations because I wanted to make a difference.

I wanted to create a company that would empower and
inspire women. I wanted to celebrate the creative souls
of women. I wanted to encourage young girls to dream
bigger dreams. I wanted to support and sustain other
women in business.

Femail Creations began as a seed, a dream to spend my days doing meaningful work. It took many years for that seed to take root. I think we all long for meaningful work, a job we can't wait to get to in the morning, a career that fulfills us, or volunteer work that matters. Some of you may know what that work is but are still feeling afraid to take the risks and do it. Others are still searching to discover what your dreams are. And, for some of you, even daring to have a dream doesn't seem possible yet. I wrote this book for all of you.

Don't Believe Everything You Hear

If you go to business school, or even just take a course or read a book, you always hear that you *have to* start with a business plan. Well, that may be the way for some people, but I have spoken with hundreds of women who started their own businesses, and many did no such thing! They may eventually end up creating a formal business plan, but that isn't really how the business began. The business actually began as a seed, a dream, a hope, a yearning, often years before the launch of the business.

They started businesses because they were passionate about something. They were passionate about creating a way to work from home, or making something they enjoyed, or providing a service they saw a need for.

There are plenty of books about how to write a business plan. But for many women that's not the place to start. Women come to me for advice or inspiration all the time, and they want to know *how I did it*. Not how I wrote a business plan, but how I discovered what my passion was. How *did* I dream up Femail Creations? How did I dare to dream that it was even possible to do it? And how did I make it happen? That's what this book is all about.

How I Dreamed Up Femail Creations

At first, I had no idea what kind of business I wanted to start. I just knew I wanted it to be meaningful to me and empowering to other women. For more than a decade, I kept a what-do-I-want-to-be-when-I-grow-up journal, filling it with ideas about just what meaningful work would look like to me. I always kept my blank book handy and filled book after book with newspaper clippings, pictures, scribbled thoughts, and any ideas I came up with for businesses I might want to start. I say if it calls to you, clip it! Sometimes you won't even be sure why an article or image resonates with you, but that doesn't matter; just trust that it does or it will someday and save it in a special place.

If you don't yet know what your dream looks like, keep a blank book handy at all times and just jot down or paste in clips of anything and everything that inspires you.

 stepping stone

I vividly recall one afternoon when I stood on my patio feeling like I was about to burst and not even really knowing why. On the outside, my life looked perfect. I had an incredible husband, two children I adored, a beautiful home, and caring friends and family. I didn't understand my feelings of discontent, and it didn't exactly help that all the people in my life thought I had "everything" a gal could want. What could possibly be missing?

I ran inside and pulled out my ratty old journal and

started flipping through the pages in search of clues. I found a newspaper clipping about an organization called the Bottomless Closet, which gathers clothing and other needed items for women returning to work. Then there was a picture torn from a magazine of a group of women gathered around a conference table together (I'm sure it was an ad for something, but in my mind they were discussing how to change the world); there was my note from back in the 1980s about the need for healthy fast food; and there was a sloppy sketch of a small cottage-like shack with a drive-through where working moms (as in *all* moms) could pick up a delicious, nutritious pot of soup and a loaf of bread made from scratch. I still wish somebody would start that business!

I discovered an old clipping for a creative retreat for novice women artists, and outlines I had once created for a women's bookstore, a gathering place for women, and a unique spa concept that was as much about community as facials. Page after page revealed that I'd been thinking about reaching out to women for a very long time. Some of the newspaper clippings were over a decade old.

The very next day I decided to start my business . . . well, not quite. I wish it were that simple! No, there was still plenty more percolating to be done. What I did decide the next day was to give myself permission to start thinking about what kind of business I might start. My blank book started filling fast; I was on fire. Whenever a thought would pop into my head, I would race to my book to jot it down. I found myself jumping out of bed in the middle of the night in search of a pen. Some of my best ideas still come to me when I am half asleep, but now I'm a little smarter. I keep a pen and paper on my nightstand – and a flashlight. Now I am ready whenever inspiration strikes.

It all starts with giving yourself permission to even think about what kind of meaningful work you might want to do.

stepping stone

Weeks went by and I just continued to allow myself to daydream about what meaningful work would look and feel like. Ideas started flowing more easily, and I noticed that just the mere thought of following my dreams made me happier. I went to the bookstore and wandered the business, art, and women's studies sections for clues on how to combine my passion for women's issues and my creative side into a business. I allowed myself a few minutes each day to read, write, or muse about my hopes and dreams. Just giving myself that permission was so liberating!

My kids would ask what we were having for dinner and I would say, "I don't know, but did you realize that women are starting businesses at a rate faster than men?" My head was full of facts and figures, and my heart was full of hope. I was starting to get energized by the notion that I could actually do something with my passion.

For years, I had tried to inspire others to follow their hearts and live their passions. For over a decade, I have been signing all of my letters to family and friends with "Dream Big." I always encouraged others to follow their dreams, and now it was time to take my own advice!

Over time, I actually got brave enough to talk about

it. Conversations with my friends and sisters were a lifeline as I became braver and braver about sticking my big toe into the uncharted waters of opening my own business. I also discovered how contagious courage can be. As I expounded on my hopes and dreams, others seemed to get braver about sharing or planting their own seeds for the future.

stepping stone

> Having a sounding board is invaluable as you go through this journey. Find a trusted friend or family member and start talking about your dreams and how you might make them come true.

The exhilarating thing was that I was taking my life into my own hands. Too often we think we are making choices for our lives, when what we are really doing is leaving our lives up to fate. I think this is especially true for women. It's easier that way. But then, when fate takes us down a difficult path, we have the nerve to complain that it wasn't where we wanted to go! Making a *conscious* decision means we have to be awake and aware of what matters most to us. And that takes work. But take it from me, it's so very worth it. As writer Grace Hansen says, "Don't be afraid your life will end; be afraid it will never begin."

Finding Your Calling

Years ago, I was at a motivational conference when the speaker asked the group what at the time seemed like a simple question. She asked us what we would do if we knew we would not fail. If we were guaranteed success, what would we attempt? I find that question to be one of the most clarifying we can ask ourselves. When we eliminate all our self-doubts and remove all our inner (and outer) critics, we have a better chance at getting at the truth.

Therein lies the answer to the age-old question: What do I want to be when I grow up? Think about it. What would *you* do if you were absolutely guaranteed success? Would you be a stand-up comic, an architect, a photographer, a social worker, a café owner, a clothes designer, a midwife? Whatever your fantasy, *that's* what you should be doing – guarantee or no guarantee.

What are you being called to do? Stop, sit, and listen for a while. The answer will come.

stepping stone

I truly believe that discovering our own passions and finding the courage to follow them are our greatest callings. When people ask me what the single most important tool is for unearthing our dreams, I tell them solitude. In order to find our authentic purpose, our passion, we have to spend lots of time listening, really listening, to ourselves. It seems so simple really, but how many of us actually do it? Our days are so overflowing with to-do lists and phone calls and emails that we rarely just unplug and hear what our hearts are telling us. At the beginning of something there has to be nothing. We have to give ourselves a clean slate – and permission to dream.

By giving myself that permission to dream, I gave birth to a company that has been one of the most worthwhile adventures of my life. My hope is that through telling my story and sharing a few of the lessons I've learned (usually the hard way!), I will inspire you to dream big, too.

creating a life of passion and purpose

1

*You may be disappointed if you fail, but you are
doomed if you don't try.* — BEVERLY SILLS

N OW THAT I HAD GIVEN MYSELF PERMISSION TO
dream and had a collage of clues scattered out
before me, I had to bring my ideas into focus. I had a
great road map and lots of signs that I was on the right
path, but now I had to make a decision. What would my
business be?

I had always dreamed of becoming a feminist philan-
thropist, someone who just gave money away to good
causes, but since I hadn't yet amassed my own fortune
and didn't have a rich aunt, let alone a rich aunt who was
about to die and leave me all of her money, I decided I'd
better go with plan B.

I knew I had to start a business that would somehow
support or empower other women. But what? The answer
seemed to arrive to me whole. Truly. One day I just woke
up and said, "I'm going to start a catalog." I love to shop –

via catalogs in my pajamas, not in a crowded mall. (My kids used to joke that without our UPS man we wouldn't have anything to wear and our house would be empty!) It was perfect. My catalog would focus on supporting women artists and other women-owned businesses, allowing me to combine my creative side with my passion for women's issues.

I had always felt strongly that we make a statement with our shopping dollars, whether we realize it or not. I go out of my way to patronize women-owned businesses. If I need shampoo, I go to Anita Roddick's Body Shop. If I need a book, I am willing to drive across town to the women's bookstore rather then buy it from the mass chains. Having a catalog whose products represented hundreds of other small businesses and individual artists would be a dream come true.

Figuring Out Where to Even Begin

Okay, so I knew I wanted to start a catalog. I didn't have a clue exactly how to go about it. Back to my blank book, which in reality was now a tall stack! I wouldn't be where I am today without spiral-bound blank books! Once again, I started jotting down ideas in a journal, mostly thoughts about what I wanted the catalog to be like rather than details about how to actually do it. I wrote down that I wanted each issue of the catalog to help a different charity. I wanted to let customers know about all the wonderful work being done by nonprofit organizations. I wanted to focus on women artists and celebrate their creativity. I wanted the catalog to be by, for, and about women. I wanted to create a community for women, and I wanted them to anticipate each issue with excitement.

Anytime I had a thought or concept, I would jot it down in my blank journal, filling page after page with ideas and bursts of inspirations.

When you're at the planning stage, keep your journal handy and jot down every idea you have – not just for how to start your business but also what your business will look and feel like and the values you want it to reflect.

stepping stone

When my sister-in-law and friend Julie called to see if I wanted to take a road trip with her, I brought along my journal and we brainstormed together. By the end of the trip, the rest of the journal was full with juicy tidbits and dreams for a catalog. Actually, I really wanted Julie to start the catalog with me – in part because she is my dear friend and I wanted her to take her own turn and have her own income, and in part because I was scared and didn't want to do it alone. For a few months, we plugged along trying to pull this off with her in one state and me in another. In the end, it was clear I would have to be brave and go it alone. As Julie once told me, she was just the midwife, I was the mother. She held my hand during the birth of the business, but now this baby was mine to raise.

Starting a business is truly a lot like giving birth. First the idea gestates, then it is born, then come the colic and sleepless nights, then the terrible two's, the bumpy teenage years, and then hopefully someday your business matures and goes off to college.

stepping stone

No Turning Back Now

When I got back from the road trip, the seeds of this idea had so firmly taken hold that I almost forgot I already had a day job. At the time, I was still managing the office side of our construction company and my husband was managing the field side of the business. We were a two-person team, working out of a two-room home office. All I could think about was getting the catalog started and what I needed to do next. I told my husband, Jeff, what I was going to do.

Knowing me better than anyone else, Jeff didn't ask how I planned to do this or what I was thinking, he simply told me he thought it was a great idea and then got the heck out of my way. I'm not sure he would have been so enthusiastic if he had known that I would soon be dumping the running of the construction office in his lap!

It was only a matter of days into the catalog business when I realized I couldn't do both jobs; there just weren't enough hours in the day – or night. My brain was in overdrive with lists, my heart was overflowing with joy at the prospect of really making a difference, and my body was oozing adrenaline. I would spring out of bed at 5:00 A.M. (bear in mind, I am *not* a morning person) and run down the hall to my home office to jot down my latest idea. After a twenty-plus-hour day, I would climb back in bed at 2:00 A.M. and start the whole thing over again.

The second week, I went into my office, boxed up everything construction related, and took it down the hall to Jeff's office. He discovered the boxes on his floor when he got home later that day. Without skipping a beat, he unpacked the boxes and put the files in his filing cabinet and started where I left off.

After a few days, Jeff popped his head into my office to ask a question about one of the projects I had just dumped into his lap. I was so completely immersed in the catalog and looking forward that I couldn't get my brain to go back. I said with a sigh, "I didn't know how to do that either when I started managing the office. Nobody showed me; I just figured it out, and I am sure you will, too."

He let out his own sigh and went back to his office. Jeff knew I was a woman on a mission and there was no going back. Once I start something, it is full steam ahead. Amazingly, he never once complained about his newly doubled workload.

Suffice it to say that I'm aware not every husband would be as supportive as Jeff. I'm very blessed indeed.

A Business Plan? What's That?

With Jeff taking on my construction office work, I was able to fully focus on the tasks at hand and the work that was piling up on my desk. I was amazed to discover how one question just led to a dozen others. Once I thought I had one piece of the puzzle figured out, I would discover an entirely new area of the mail-order business I hadn't even thought of yet.

This stream of inquiries continued to guide me down the river of cataloging. Sometimes this river was filled with rapids, sometimes gurgling whitewater, and sometimes a full-on waterfall – just when I least expected to be going over the edge of a cliff.

The truth is when I started down this road, I didn't have the foggiest idea how to launch a catalog. I simply knew I would burst open at the seams if I didn't create work that was meaningful to me. When the idea of a mail-order catalog finally gelled, I jumped.

I would love to say I spent months mapping out the perfect business plan. The truth is my goals were very clear, but my business plan wasn't even on a scratch piece of paper when I decided to start Femail Creations. I wasn't even sure what exactly a business plan was.

stepping stone

You don't have to know what you are doing to start to do it!

Getting Started

I began by going through my own home and picking out items that meant something to me – everything from a favorite T-shirt to a pair of earrings to a book, sculpture, or piece of art given to me by a friend. Then I set out to track down the artist behind it. I became a regular super-sleuth, and my collection continued to grow. Pretty soon, I could find an artist anywhere. And the network just continued to grow. One artist would tell me about another who made some wonderful something that would be perfect for the catalog. This phone chain greatly added to the diversity of merchandise offered, even in that first catalog.

Amazingly enough, I didn't receive a single "no" from any of the artists I called. Every artist and vendor I contacted was excited about jumping on board. That fact alone kept my spirits high and let me know that women were hungry for something just like this.

Naming the Baby

Now if only I could figure out a name for my baby. Back to the journal for inspiration. I had several ideas, and I continually bounced them off family and friends to get their reaction. One night while I was making dinner it came to me: *Femail Creations.* I said it out loud and instantly loved the words. Females in the mail! I immediately picked up the phone to call Julie. She loved it, as did everyone else. That night Femail Creations started taking on a life of her own.

My Copy Writing "Gimmick" – Not!

Now the catalog had a name, it had a mission, and it had merchandise. It seemed logical that the next step would be to start writing the descriptions for the items I was going to sell. I could barely type, and I certainly hadn't done any professional copy writing before. But I did know how to talk, so I decided to just write as if we were having a conversation. I talked and Julie typed and together we ad-libbed our way through, while Jeff served us up margaritas. That's how the copy for the first catalog was written.

I still write the catalog today in that same informal and personal way. I just write down a little something about each product and artist as if I were telling it to an old friend. I'm not the Kathy Lee of cataloging, but I do mention my family and my dog, Zoë, from time to time. If my son happens to walk in and say something about a product while I'm writing copy, chances are it will end up in the catalog, too. If my sister is with me when I find a new product, or if it's 3:00 A.M. and I'm still up scrambling to make a production deadline, I'll probably mention that in the copy, too.

I once went to press with text for one item that basically said, "It's really, really late and I am out of witty adjectives. You are just going to have to trust me on this one and buy it to see for yourself how great this really is." The printer was so surprised by that sentence that she called to see if I'd left in the "dummy copy" (that's what we call the text that is used to fill the proper amount of space until final copy is written), but nope, I told her to roll the presses, that *was* the correct copy. This honest, first-person style and tell-it-like-it-is prose has actually become part of our brand. But it still comes from the heart.

I have written catalog copy just about everywhere. It is one of my jobs that I just have to squeeze in where I can. I have been known to pull out my laptop at my son's tennis matches, in the car (as a passenger, not a driver!), on many airplanes, and in hotel rooms all across the country.

Years into the business, I attended a catalog conference, and to my utter amazement, my copy was used as an example for creative branding. They thought I was a genius to come up with such a great "gimmick" for the copy. Little did they know my writing style came out of my ignorance about how copy *should* be written.

"Branding"

From the night the name came to me I was determined to have a very distinct logo for Femail Creations. I didn't have anything specific in mind, but I knew it had to be original. Since I can't even draw a stick figure, I knew I wouldn't be the one to come up with it, so I called a local artist who had done a unique project for me years before. Since she hadn't found my last request strange – to have prose from one of my favorite books painted on my family room wall – I knew she had the creative mindset I was looking for.

I gave her the name and brainstormed with her a little bit, and in a matter of days, she came back with this beautiful wild woman, with long flowing curly hair and a passionate attitude, dancing in celebration of the creative souls of women. I loved it instantly.

Several months later, I was having lunch with this same artist, and while driving home I told her again how much I loved the logo and how everyone commented on her wild curly hair. She turned to me in the car with this weird look on her face. She said, "*Her* curly hair? That's *your* curly hair! Of course I based *your* logo on *you*." I was stunned. How could I have been looking at this logo for months and not known that I was the inspiration for it? I think the only person more shocked than I was, was the artist. She couldn't believe I hadn't realized it.

The fact is when we first met I did indeed have long curly hair. But starting a business can literally make you pull your hair out. Ha! So I had cut off my locks in favor of a shorter, faster-drying style. I guess having short hair and being worn out from working so many hours had blinded me to the resemblance. Discovering that I was the inspiration for the logo gave me something to laugh about and a reminder not to lose touch with that part of myself.

Learning the Production Ropes

Once I had gathered up what, in my inexperience, I deemed to be enough merchandise to fill a catalog, I decided the next thing to do would be to find a photographer. Almost immediately, new words like *stylist* and *props* started coming up, but there wasn't any money in the budget for that, so it was wing-it time once again.

One foot in front of the other, I just groped my way along. Of course, there were a few jobs I couldn't handle myself. For starters, the photographer asked me questions about color separations and design. I had no idea why colors need to be separated, but I knew I'd better find someone who did. Then, the color separator asked me who would be doing the graphic design and layout for the catalog. In those days, I didn't know Quark from Cuisinart. In fact, I was a techno peasant who had only owned a computer for about a year or two and was still just using it as a glorified typewriter.

Layout. I needed to do the layout. I found some poster board lying around the house, no doubt left over from one of the kid's school projects, and cut and pasted the photos onto it. I began by deciding what would go on which page and then just glued the images to the poster board. I later learned this was called pagination – and it certainly wasn't done with poster board and Elmer's glue! But my homegrown technique got me through that phase of the first catalog, and in fact many more to come.

The color separator referred me to a graphic artist and I gave her my makeshift poster-board layouts so she could start putting them in the computer in the proper file format and prepare them for the printer. The artist who designed the logo stepped in and helped me with sketches for what I was calling our storyboards. People were just so generous and just guided me along. Seeing those first color proofs of the catalog was beyond exciting and made the project start to seem real.

I plugged along, continuing to pick up knowledge about the mail-order business as I went. After spending weeks researching order-entry software, I decided to purchase Mail Order Manager, or MOM, as we called her, to process the orders. MOM became the software for all of the functions of the catalog.

Finding Office Space

I was still running things from my kitchen table at this point, but it was clear I couldn't continue doing that for long. Jeff and I decided it made the most sense to find office space we could share and at long last get the construction company out of our house. So we found a space that seemed plenty big and was ready for immediate occupancy – and that was key, since we wanted to move in as soon as possible.

My to-do list seemed never ending. There were business licenses to get, bank accounts to open, mail permits to acquire, merchant services to establish, meetings with my accountant to make sure I was doing my paperwork properly for tax purposes, trademarks to register, and a million other things I didn't even know I was supposed to be doing but just learned about as I went. I was overwhelmed by all I had to do, and all I didn't know. Every day brought a dozen more things to add to my list. I was starting to understand the meaning of panic in a way I never had before.

I finally discovered that when I was feeling truly over-whelmed, relief could be found by finding at least one project on my list that could be completed in a relatively short amount of time. It might not even be the most important item on my list, but the sense of accomplishment made it worth doing first. Getting to cross even one thing off the list made a difference.

stepping stone

> Yard by yard, life really is hard; inch by inch, life can be a cinch.

When it came time to place purchase orders for the initial inventory, I had a bit of a panic attack. How was I supposed to know how many of each item we would sell? We certainly didn't have any money to waste, and I felt a lot of pressure to get this part right. It seemed like I was just throwing darts trying to determine how much product to order. It definitely felt more like a guessing game than an educated guess. Because this was the first catalog, I didn't have any historical data to guide me, and I had no idea how to forecast which items would be the best sellers and which ones would tank. (I know, I know. If I *had* known, none of them would have tanked, right?)

I later learned that there is a general rule in cataloging known as the "one-third, one-third, and one-third rule," meaning that one-third of the items in a catalog will be dogs (very poor sellers), one-third will be middle-of-the-road sellers, and one-third will be winners. Over the years, I have certainly had my share of dogs, and fortunately, my share of surprise winners as well.

Printing and Mailing the First Catalog

The next big question was who was going to print the catalog. I didn't know thing one about printing either, and
I was worried about having to learn yet another new set
of terms and negotiating yet another costly contract.

I was fortunate to find a local printer who took me
under her wing and showed me the ropes. Christy Creel
gave me a clinic in printing terminology and taught me the
difference between forty-pound paper and fifty-pound
paper and varying degrees of whiteness, and she even met
me at the press in the middle of the night to review color
with me. Eventually we outgrew Creel Printing, but the
education and support Christy provided was invaluable
and greatly appreciated.

It was Christy who asked me who would be mailing the
catalogs. Looking back it is hard to believe that I made
it that far without considering who would be mailing the
catalogs – and to whom we would be mailing them. List
rental was another uncharted area for me. I didn't know
there was such a thing or that you could actually rent
people's names.

Since I considered myself to be my own demographic,
I looked through my own bedside basket of catalogs and
magazines and, after picking five or ten publications I
thought would be compatible, I contacted each one to
see if they in fact rented their lists. Some did, some didn't,
and others referred me to their list manager or broker.
After a few days on the phone, I secured enough names
for our first mailing of thirty thousand catalogs. I can't
say a lot of research went into determining that thirty
thousand was the right number. The truth is that the

number was chosen strictly for financial reasons. Between printing costs and renting lists and paying for the mailing, that's how many I could afford. Later I would learn that circulation (knowing which lists to rent, how many catalogs to send out and when) is a science all unto itself and a key part of a successful catalog.

I was vaguely aware that postage would be a hefty percentage of my (nonexistent) budget, but writing that first huge check almost stopped my heart. Uncle Sam doesn't offer terms. You pay for your postage up front or your catalogs don't get mailed. Cha Ching! Before I even had a chance to sell a single item from the catalog, I had already paid for a photographer, color separations, a graphic artist, some of the inventory, and a whole lot of postage – and I had a big printing tab waiting in the wings. I was quickly learning just how capital-intensive a cataloging business really is.

It's probably just as well I didn't know beforehand. If I had, I'm not sure I would have had the guts to start. Sometimes ignorance really *is* bliss.

stepping stone

Sometimes it is a good thing you don't know what you don't know.

taking our turn

2

The jump is so frightening between where I am and where I want to be . . . because of all I may become, I will close my eyes and leap!

— MARY ANNE RACHMACHER

SO, THAT'S HOW MY STORY BEGINS. I DECIDED TO take my turn and then leaped into the unknown. It felt foreign to me to put myself at the top of my list. As women we have been so conditioned our entire lives to put everyone else's needs first that we seem to have some kind of innate sense of guilt about putting our own needs at the top of the list even just once in a while. The mere thought of allowing our passions to *show up* on our to-do lists can feel like some kind of sin, not to mention putting them first! Yet doing just that is one of the most important things we will ever do.

This I know for sure: Only you can take your turn. If you have a dream, or are struggling to define your dream, go for it. No one else will do it for you. Nobody else can put you at the top of your own list.

stepping stone

We exhaust ourselves trying to be all things to all people – all people but ourselves! We even forget that we *have* needs; they are buried under so many layers of "shoulds."

I hear from many women who want to take their turn but are faced with what I call the "as long as" syndrome – the idea that it is okay for her to start her own business "as long as" dinner is still on the table at the usual time, "as long as" she still drives the kids to every soccer game or piano lesson, the house remains spotless, the laundry still gets done, and so on. "As long as" nobody in the household is inconvenienced, sure, go ahead. Such expectations stop too many of us from becoming fully who we are meant to be.

We women have to learn how to take as good care of ourselves as we do others – to extend that same boundless love and compassion to ourselves that we do to our partners and kids. Sure, it can be hard, but taking our turn and peeling back the layers to find our passions and unearth our dreams is worth every bit of effort it will take.

stepping stone

For a day, a week, a month, try putting yourself first. Notice what gets in your way and try to remove your obstacles. It'll be a real eye-opener.

Getting to Know Yourself

When I asked my friend and artist Marlo Miyashiro how she learned to put herself first she said:

> I was taught the concept "consideration" early on in my life. I was expected to put other peoples' needs, wants, and desires before my own. . . . It wasn't until I embraced

my independence that I realized that the only way to truly care for others was to make sure that my own needs were taken care of so that I would have the energy and confidence to help others. It is a difficult lesson that I still work with every day.

I may be keenly aware of how important that is – but I'm certainly a long way from actually being there. Learning to love and accept ourselves is a lifelong process, isn't it?

What would you do if you did indeed love yourself? How would your life look different? What dreams might you be following?

 stepping stone

A lot of women stop themselves because they don't think they're creative. Well, creativity comes in many forms; we're all creative souls. I think we tend to overlook that fact. Whether we create a sculpture, a collage, a garden, a dinner cooked with love, a letter that makes a friend smile, or a better place to live or work, we are creating. I certainly can't draw or paint or make much of anything, but it was my creativity that gathered together those who could and created a home for their handcrafted work in a mail-order catalog. We need to discover what makes our juices flow, but from there the sky's the limit. I find that more often than not women don't take their turn because they're out of touch with their own passions.

Think about where you put your own creativity to use. You might not even notice because it comes so naturally. Is it in how you dress? How you decorate your home? In your volunteer work? In

 stepping stone

> *how you play with your kids? Don't belittle it*
> *because it comes easily. Honor your creativity.*

Acting on Our Passions

Believe me, I used not knowing what I wanted to do as an excuse for not doing it for a long time. At some point, I realized that I was the only one who could determine my direction and that I'd better do something about it. And so I began journaling and creating collages to find the common thread among the things that I felt drawn to.

Then, once I knew what I wanted my meaningful work to accomplish, I allowed not knowing exactly what *kind* of business could achieve that result to stop me. When the light bulb finally came on and I realized that I was the only one stopping me, I was out of excuses. I had to decide whether or not to take my turn and commit to following my passion. That was a very frightening time.

Like so many other women I've encountered along the way, I had been hiding behind my identity as a wife and mother instead of finding the courage to listen to that voice inside that kept calling me to act upon my passions. But once you connect with that voice, it demands to be heard. Ultimately, it leaves you with two choices: act or live with the regret that you didn't. The first requires courage, the second brings sorrow. Both may seem difficult, but finding courage to take our turn is the only choice that leads to satisfaction, or at the very least to the satisfaction in knowing we dared to try.

When I asked artist Lori Rodgers what advice she would give women about living out loud and following their dreams she said:

Do not listen to or befriend people who say you can't do it or you are too old or whatever. Surround yourself with strong, loving friends who support your dreams and go for the top! If you fail . . . get up and go again.

Gaining Courage

I have had many people tell me how grateful they are for Femail Creations and the great source of inspiration it is in their lives. Some have asked me how I found the courage. Actually, starting my own business required more courage than I thought I had, and many days it still does. In my case, it's the feedback I get from customers that fuels me; it gives me the courage to continue. It's really a big, wonderful circle. The more I meet my own need to fly, the more I meet the needs of my customers, the more they appreciate what I do, the more courage I feel, and the more I meet my own need to fly, and on and on.

Lori Bugaj, one of the artists in the catalog, shared her insight and what working with Femail Creations has meant to her.

Femail Creations has touched me in many different ways. As a customer, I have never found a greater source of beautiful and inspiring gifts just for women than what Lisa provides in every issue. As an artist, working with Lisa and her whole team at Femail Creations has been strange! Lisa is fun. There is no pretense; there is no ulterior motive; there are no hidden agendas. Femail Creations is one of the greatest champions of women and women's causes that I have known. Lisa does not compromise: She does not compromise her vision of what her company is and will be. If she wants to give proceeds and profits to help others, no one's going to get in her way. She does not compromise her artists. She doesn't take advantage of us by selling our ideas or our products to the cheapest bidder overseas. She believes in us and wants to see each and every one of us succeed. But most importantly, each time I see her, Lisa proves to me that business can be personal. That it can be feminine – emotional, caring, loving. That we, as women who own businesses, do not have to live by the rules set forth by the "old boys club." Lisa and Femail Creations prove to me that I can do what I want, how I want. You just don't find that in other businesses!

In short, knowing that I have inspired others to follow their own dreams or shown other women that you can indeed run a business with heart and soul has made the risk of taking my turn worth *all* the fear I have had to face. As we commit to ourselves and our own vision, we reap the rewards of inspiring others. As we take our turn, we inspire others to do the same; and there is no greater reward than that.

learning how to fly

3

Life is either a daring adventure or nothing at all. — HELEN KELLER

BACK TO MY STORY...
At first we ran our construction company, Hammond Caulking Inc., and Femail Creations out of our home. As anyone with a home-based business knows, working from home has its advantages and disadvantages. Having an office at home means you can work whenever you want without having to get dressed or get into your car for a drive to the office. However, with the office right there it is always a challenge to *stop* working. It's too easy to keep going round the clock.

Different things work for different people. I know people who try to work from home who are constantly distracted or always find something better (more fun) to do and consequently don't get any work done. I find that working from home successfully takes a lot of self-motivation and self-discipline. I certainly don't recommend it for everyone. Some people need the structure of an office to stay on track; others need the contact that comes with working with other people and find working from home isolating. Personally, I work very well from home and find that it is the space I work best in when I am focusing on the creative side of my business. I tend to do the left-brain projects in the main office and the right brain projects in my home office.

Our First "Real" Office and Our First Employee

Eventually it became clear that we needed more space. I must say, moving into an office made the catalog business feel all that much more real. Our first office was only about 800 square feet. We had a reception area, an office for Jeff, and one for me, and an open area for the inventory.

It soon became clear that despite my best efforts there weren't enough hours in the day for one person to get everything done. So we contemplated hiring our first employee. As luck would have it, my mom, who tends to move frequently, just happened to be in between the three or four cities she rotates through and was game to help. So my mom became our first employee. We helped her move to our neck of the woods, and we became an office of three.

Our First Order!

The maiden issue of Femail Creations was in the mail, and orders were finally starting to come in. I still remember how exciting it was when that first order came in! I loved answering the order line and talking with the customers, then I would carefully pick and pack each order. I would stack the boxes up by the front door so they would be ready for Benny, our office UPS driver. More and more calls came in, and orders started to arrive by mail and fax. It was nothing short of thrilling for us when Benny brought in the dolly to haul the boxes out to the truck – that meant we had more orders shipping out than Benny could carry in his arms! Some days I swear Benny brought in the dolly just to humor us. He was a pretty strong guy, and I am sure he could easily manage the five or six boxes without the dolly, but he knew how excited we got.

The dolly became our benchmark for a successful day. It was a big shipping day if Benny needed the dolly! I laugh looking back on those days. Years later, it would require a semi-truck to haul away a day's worth of orders, but back then, we got excited about the dolly.

The Next Catalog? So Soon?

Soon the customers started asking about when the next catalog would be coming out. The next one? I hadn't even caught my breath from the first one, but fall was just around the corner, and I knew we couldn't continue sending out a spring-themed catalog in the fall. Not many people would want to buy summer products once the leaves started changing. I figured this next catalog would be easier because this time I knew a little more. I was about to learn just how little I really knew.

The main problem with the second catalog was that the first catalog hadn't generated enough orders to pay for it! With all of my budget (I use that term loosely as I didn't exactly have a formal budget yet) spent and very little revenue coming in, I would have to get creative about financing round two.

It was around this time that I learned one of the big

cosmic jokes: banks will only loan you money if you don't need it. When you haven't shown a profit yet, you aren't considered a good risk. No profit, no loan for you! By the time you have some positive cash flow, banks will fall all over themselves to loan you money.

Getting by on Loans, Credit Cards, Second Mortgages

With no hope of a business loan and savings quickly running out, it seemed the only thing left to do was mortgage our house. The mere thought of doing this scared the hell out of me, of course. I hated to put the roof over my family's head on the line for my dream. But it was my only resource for the capital I so badly needed to continue, thanks to my serious miscalculation about how much money it would take to launch a catalog. It would be years before I would realize just how many zeros off I had been.

I applied for a business credit card, asked the vendors to extend terms, and planned to do more myself to reduce costs. I asked Jeff to help me with the photo shoots so we could work faster. He ironed the clothes we were photographing, helped set up the next shot, and became my prop master and right arm at the exhausting photo shoots. Since we paid by the day instead of the shot, we kept those photographers hopping! They used to complain that we didn't even give them lunch breaks.

On one photo shoot, we were getting ready to photograph some doggie treats we were going to sell in the catalog. As I set the shot up, Bob, one of the photographers, decided to try them out for himself. I will never forget the look on Jeff's face when he realized what Bob was doing. Much to our amazement and amusement Bob dipped his doggie treat in ranch dressing and declared it delicious. We kidded him for years about that.

I knew I couldn't afford a graphic artist this time around, so I decided to save money and buy the software and do it myself. There was just one problem: I don't read instructions. I think there are basically two kinds of people in the world: those who read the directions and those who don't. I'm definitely in the later category.

I am a visual person – show me how to do it and I am just fine – just don't make me read the instruction manual. My mom, however, did read directions, so her first assignment was to read the software manual and show me how to run it. She was a huge help. I can't say the early versions of the catalogs I did were works of art, but they sufficed, and the customers didn't complain. Luckily, there aren't many copies left of those first few catalogs, and most of those are in my garage!

Moving Offices Again . . .

We were only in our first office for a few months when it became clear we had seriously underestimated the amount of space we were going to need. It cost us so much to get out of our lease that it was downright depressing. Then, on a Friday, the last day of our move, the office was broken into and all of our computers and the phone system were stolen.

We were pretty sure we knew who had done it and told the police about our suspicions. After an investigation, the police agreed with our theory but were never able to get enough evidence to prosecute. That was only the beginning of our bad luck . . . we had let the insurance lapse a day too early at the old office and none of the stolen equipment was going to be covered. To add insult to injury, we lost all of our data and consequently our customer list.

I didn't know what to do, so I called my brother Brian, a self-taught computer genius and webmaster and asked him if he could please come down and help us get a new computer system back up and running – by Monday. Brian only lived a few hours away, and he got in his car (it felt like a white horse to us) and came down to help us put the pieces back together. He built a few new computers for us and got the network set up at the new office for us in forty-eight hours. We learned a lot of costly lessons during this move; we were never again underinsured or without a backup system for our computers.

When we finally got the second catalog done and in the mail, UPS unexpectedly went on strike. Now maybe there were some businesses that expected it, but Femail Creations wasn't one of them. We were affected both coming and going. As orders started coming in, we couldn't keep a reliable inventory because our vendors used UPS, and we couldn't ship orders because we used UPS to fulfill our orders, too.

Fortunately, in times of crisis I tend to skip the panic and jump into action. The US Postal Service had just unveiled their new Priority Mail service, so I called them. I thought that might be a good option to solve our current crisis. They were so gung ho to get businesses signed up for their new service that they even offered us free boxes and tape.

Now I realize for most businesses that wouldn't be that big of a deal, but for a mail-order catalog, it was a very big deal! That would be a huge cost saving for us. So we switched from shipping most of our packages UPS to shipping them with USPS. What started out as a disaster ended up being a blessing in disguise and saved us lot of money in the long run.

> *What often looks like a disaster at first can sometimes turn out to be a blessing in disguise. Bad news can really be good news in the long run.*

stepping stone

And Then Moving Again . . .

Only a few months into our move to a second office, it was clear that I had screwed up again. It seemed big enough when we moved in, honest it did, but it became evident pretty quickly that even this 1700-square-foot space wasn't going to be big enough to accommodate all of the inventory and give us the room we needed for shipping. There was enough room for the inventory when it was on the shelves, but not for all of the boxes of filled orders waiting to ship out. I couldn't stomach another move, so I called the landlord and asked him if we could perhaps increase the size of our current space. Luck was on our side this time, and the unit next to us was empty so we just knocked down a wall and expanded. Now we had a designated area for shipping.

With the catalog being more than a full-time job – in fact more than two full-time jobs – Jeff was picking up my slack at home and it was becoming clear that he was going to need help managing the construction business. My brother Brad was a perennial favorite around our house, having lived with us from time to time between his college and military days. My kids adored him, and Jeff and Brad always got along well, so I suggested that Jeff give Brad a call. Brad and his wife, Nina, who was pregnant with their first child at the time, lived in Park City, Utah. Jeff offered Brad the job of Field Superintendent, and Brad accepted, so Brad and Nina moved to Las Vegas and joined the clan.

Our First Holiday Issue

Meanwhile, I was diving into the design of my third catalog – the all-important holiday issue. This being our first one, I had no idea just how key the holiday season was for a gift catalog. I figured the sales from this catalog would be higher because people would be shopping for gifts, I just didn't realize how much higher.

In just a few weeks after Brad started working for Hammond Caulking, I mailed my first holiday catalog. The phones almost immediately started ringing off the hook, and I was scrambling around the clock to take the orders and then ship them out. My mom had already moved back to the next city on her rotation, and it was just me again. I told Jeff I was going to have to "borrow" Brad for a few weeks just to help me get caught up. Of course, a few weeks turned into a few months, and Brad never did get back to working for Hammond Caulking.

It was clear we needed even more help, so I put an ad in the paper for an administrative assistant to help answer the phones. The irony, of course, was that putting the ad in the paper just made the phone ring even more! I asked Brad if Nina might like to come down and help answer phones for a while until we got this position filled. She agreed, and at least I had a temporary solution. Nina took all of the local calls and screened the résumés so I could start interviewing the applicants.

After several dismal interviews, I was starting to get worried. Although Nina was overqualified for the position, I went ahead and asked her if she would like to stay around for a few months as our administrative assistant. She wasn't due until February, and I figured that with her help we might just make it through that first holiday season.

It was a three-ring circus at the office, with the phones ringing nonstop. Jeff would work all day and then go home and pick up the kids and dinner and head to the office so we could all eat together. The kids would get their homework done, help us pack up a few orders, and then Jeff would take them home to tuck them in, often returning to work the "graveyard" shift with Brad and Nina and me. Jeff spent so many hours helping me in shipping that when our then seven-year-old son brought home a story he had written about his family for school, it said that his daddy worked for his mommy and didn't mention the fact that Jeff owned a construction company at all.

Our family truly lived at the office. Taking calls by day and shipping orders by night became our routine for months. Sleep didn't seem to be on the agenda. Nina was right there with us. I have never seen a pregnant woman with so much energy!

The week before Christmas, orders finally started slowing down. Of course, the phone still had to be answered twenty-four hours a day. Jeff and I would take shifts so we could spend time with the kids decorating the tree and trying to squeeze in some merriment amongst the mayhem. I finally got the kids to sleep around midnight on Christmas Eve, then headed back to the office to relieve Jeff. We only took a few calls that night, but to me every customer mattered. I felt that way then and I feel that way today.

On Christmas morning Jeff got up early to take the 5:00 A.M. shift with the phones. Back then, Jeff was a low-tech kind of fellow and couldn't actually enter the orders directly into the system, so he would try to juggle the phone while writing down the orders on paper. It was quite a sight, with his head kinked to hold the phone between his shoulder and his ear and his free hand manually taking the order, all the while trying to charm his way through the product questions.

They say behind every good man is a great woman. Well, let me tell you, behind this woman and this catalog is a great man! I couldn't have done this without his support.

Around 9:00 A.M. on Christmas morning we couldn't hold the kids at bay any longer, so we left the phones unattended to be home as a family for a few hours and open presents around the tree. After a big breakfast, we all returned to the office together. The kids brought down all of their new holiday toys to keep them entertained, I answered the 800 number and entered the orders Jeff had taken earlier, while he got us caught up in shipping. In the end, we only took about a dozen calls that day, but we were grateful for each and every order.

Talking to Customers

Customers were always shocked when they discovered that it was me on the other end of the phone, and even more surprised when I told them I would be the one picking and packing their order as well. One night I got my own surprise when I discovered Riane Eisler, the author of the incredible *The Chalice and the Blade,* on the other end of the line. What a thrill that was! Not only did I get to speak with her, but she was shopping at Femail Creations!

Over the years, I have had the pleasure of taking catalog orders for stars like Jadda Pinkett Smith and Kathy Najimy. Our first really big order came from Jadda Pinkett Smith, who was doing some of her Christmas shopping at Femail Creations. She will probably never know how much it meant to us to have her support. When Kathy Najimy purchased one of our Girls Rock T-shirts, she loved it so much she wore it on several of her TV appearances and got the entire cast of Veronica's Closet to wear them on an episode of that show! When I wrote to thank her and tell her my daughter actually designed that shirt, she sent me a thank-you note right back for my vision to start a company like Femail Creations.

Frankly, I loved talking with the customers and hearing how excited they were about the catalog. I am always amazed to hear that other companies don't take the time to listen. The customers always share such invaluable insight into what they like and don't like. To this day, some of our best ideas come from them.

My nephew Ethan was born in February, but that didn't put Nina out of commission for long. Soon after our bundle of joy arrived, she was back at work with him in tow. Ethan spent his first few months of life hanging out with us at the office. It gave me the chance to bond with him – or, as my sisters will tell you, brainwash him into believing I am his favorite aunt!

He was so cute and there was never a shortage of open

arms waiting to hold him. When my kids got out of school in the afternoons, they couldn't wait to get to the office to play with Ethan. When it was nap time, the bins in shipping were the perfect size for a sleeping baby. When he outgrew the warehouse containers, his favorite aunt went out and bought a playpen for the office. When he got a little more active, we hung a swing from the office door for him to bounce up and down in. When he outgrew that, we got him a walker to cruise up and down the halls. I am sure this kind of arrangement wouldn't have been possible in most offices, but in a small company with all of the employees related it worked.

stepping stone

When it's your company, you get to make – and break – the rules!

In between taking calls and shipping boxes, I was placing purchase orders for more inventory, working with the vendors to come up with new merchandise ideas, shuffling the paperwork, paying the bills, and starting on the next catalog – always the next catalog. There is truly never a break between catalogs. One deadline collides with the next.

My First "Real" Employee

It was time to hire my first "real" employee – in other words someone who wasn't actually related to me! Jeff had finally hired some office help, and I could see what a difference it made in his ability to focus on the bigger picture of running a business. I had been winging it for a year and a half, and now I either needed to clone myself or hire some help. After putting an ad in the paper, I hired Emma* to help manage things and take some of the operational issues off my plate.

I should have known she wasn't a good fit from the very first day, when she seemed a bit put out about having to share an office. When she interviewed she should have noticed our tight quarters. I didn't even have my own office. Why would she think she would? Welcome to the world of small business. Emma seemed more worried about breaking a nail than about getting the orders shipped and the boxes out the door.

When it came time to move again – yes I know, I blew it again! – Emma wanted to know which moving company she should contact. Moving company? You are looking at your movers! Of course, she was shocked that we'd be moving ourselves and carefully explained how, at her last job, when they moved, everyone just packed up their personal things and put them in the special box the company provided and set that on their desk, and the moving company did everything else. Then, when everyone arrived back at work, their files were all put away and their desks and computers were set up and ready to go.

Well, isn't that nice? I explained to her that things would be working a little differently here. Here everyone would be given a stack of cardboard boxes and a tape gun and we would all work together until everything was moved and set up at the new office – by us! Having Emma around gave me my first, but certainly not my last, insight into the difference between big business and small business.

The third office was plenty big. I had finally learned my lesson and made sure we not only had enough room

* Some of the names in this book have been changed to protect the innocent, and the not so innocent who can afford good attorneys.

to fit everything, but plenty of room to grow. I had also learned my lesson about the high costs of getting out of a lease. This time I called the landlord and negotiated a bigger space within the same complex, thereby avoiding early termination of a lease. I designed the new space to include a call center (I had finally realized that I couldn't personally answer the 800 number forever) and a shipping area, with several offices for the staff that I didn't have yet but hopefully soon would, and for the construction company staff, which was also expanding in size. We even had a break room and a conference room now. It felt more like a real office and gave us the opportunity to get better organized.

Starting the Call Center

Now that we had some place for them to sit, we could finally hire people to answer our 800 numbers for orders and customer service. Having a call center proved to be, well, let's just say a very *interesting* experience. I don't know what it is about that environment, but ask anyone about working in or running a call center and I assure you they will have some stories to tell. The first employee we hired for the call center was actually found sleeping under her desk one morning when Brad arrived at the office. She was supposed to be covering the early-morning shift for the phones but had decided to make a little bed under her desk instead and catch some shuteye. We gave her a second chance and she turned out to be a great employee in many ways; however, starting early in the morning was never one of them.

We had a real cast of characters in there. One guy we hired thought his cell phone calls took precedence over answering the 800 number. As you can imagine, he didn't last too long around there. One woman must have been convinced she was going to starve to death and constantly hid food – think Costco-sized tubs of it – behind every binder, under every folder, and in every drawer. When the office became infested with so many ants they could have filmed the sequel to the *Antz* movie, we finally had to put a no-food-allowed rule into place for the call center.

But we should have gone even further and included a no drinking rule too! A few months after our ant invasion, one of the gals in the call center spilled her Coke all over her keyboard and it ran down the desk into the hard drive of her computer, ruining the machine.

We thought that after that it would be pretty clear to everyone working in the call center why drinks at your desk were not such a good idea. Wrong! One staff member had eighteen – no, that wasn't a typo – huge, plastic, refillable cups at her work station. I have never understood why anyone needs a gallon-drum-sized drink from 7-Eleven, but apparently this woman needed eighteen of them!

We had all of the usual issues call centers tend to face, from the typical problem of gossip to the rare problem of hygiene. Nobody wants to sit next to somebody who smells or has bad breath. But with June things were extreme. After gift baskets of soap and bath gel went unnoticed and the staff started spraying her chair with Febreze, it came time to have a talk about her bathing – or lack thereof – rituals. Always a delicate matter to have to discuss, and never any fun. I certainly don't recall seeing that in my job description! Thank heaven I had my sister Diane to commiserate with. She'd been a supervisor in a call center and knew all about how weird things can get.

Next Came the Warehouse

Hiring our first warehouse employees to help out with shipping seemed to go a little smoother. I loved working in the warehouse. It was the one area where you could actually get a real sense of accomplishment in a short amount of time. When you spent a few hours picking and packing orders, there was a big pile of boxes stacked up allowing you to see the fruits of your labor. When producing the catalog or keeping up on all of the paperwork, it never seemed like I was getting anything done, no matter how hard I worked. With catalog production, I wouldn't see the fruits of hours and hours of work until the thing printed and mailed many months later. And paperwork is like dishes and laundry – it's never ending. When I needed a break from the mental side of the business, I would throw on my jeans and a sweatshirt and head back into the shipping area to fulfill orders.

Jeff and I frequently spent the graveyard shift together in the warehouse. I would gather the items for each order and Jeff would package them up in boxes. With no interruptions and the late night adrenaline flowing between the two of us, we could pick and pack about five hundred orders a night, ironically about what our day shift of five could do. We have always moved faster than most people, whether we were walking, eating, talking, or working.

My First Convention

As we headed into our second year, it was clear we needed to work smarter, not harder. I had heard that there was going to be a Direct Marketing Convention for the mail-order catalog industry in Boston and thought it might be nice to learn a little more about this crazy business from the so-called experts. I decided that Jeff and Brad and Emma and I would all go to Boston for the convention.

But before we even made it to the convention, it was clear I would have to let Emma go. She just wasn't working, literally. I had already purchased her plane ticket, so I called the airline to ask for a refund. HA! That wasn't going to happen. The agent did tell me that if I provided a letter stating that Emma had been fired, I could at least change the name on the plane ticket so somebody else could go. Small consolation considering I didn't have any other employees to go. Having a large family was starting to come in handy.

My sister Diane was between jobs, and I knew she would go if I explained my predicament. So I called her up and asked her if she would fly to Boston with us to cover the conference track Emma was supposed to be attending. Diane was game for a road trip, and since she got the Mensa brain in our family, she was certainly better able to understand the science of circulation, and the benchmarks and statistics of fulfillment than I could.

Before we left for the convention, I spent hours studying the catalog of classes and workshops, trying to decide whom to send to which ones. There were tracks on catalog production, circulation, fulfillment, creative, merchandising, e-commerce, and executive forums. I wanted to make sure we had all of our bases covered. I carefully mapped out who would go to what so that at any given hour of the day one of us would be covering all of the key topics.

Everybody was assigned a color-coded schedule and told to stick to it. I admit I got a little obsessive about the whole thing. I am sure Brad and Diane and Jeff were all having a few good laughs about how militant I was being. But I was going to be sure we got our money's worth! I have my dad to thank for that. When I was a kid, you could count on my family to be the first ones to arrive and the last ones to leave any activity that cost money. No matter how tired and hot we might be, there was no leaving until the park closed. Didn't want to miss anything we had paid for. In that same spirit, I didn't want to miss learning something important at our first convention, and besides, it cost us a small fortune to go.

Our tight budget only allowed for one hotel room. So the four of us crammed into the tiny room – thank heaven we were all family! There was no room for a rollaway so it got real cozy with two in each bed. Brad and Diane both snored so loud that Jeff and I would throw pillows at them all night trying desperately to get them to stop. The beds were so small it was all we could do not to fall out onto the floor.

We would start early each morning after very little sleep and make our way to the convention center. Again, we weren't going to miss anything! Everyone would head to the assigned track, and then we would meet back up for lunch and have a fast and furious discussion about what we had just learned. Diane would try to explain what RFM was, while I was saying RF what? (It would be a long time before I fully understood RFM – how Recently a customer had shopped, how Frequently they shopped, and what their Monetary value was.) Brad would tell us about new manifesting systems for the warehouse and update us on the industry benchmarks we weren't even close to being able to measure, let alone meet. Jeff would reiterate that according to the numbers, we would never make money in this crazy business, and I would expound on the virtues of merchandising and how important it is to the success of a catalog. Mostly we just all talked at once and shoveled our food in so fast we barely tasted it so we could stay on schedule and make it to the next class.

At the end of each very long day, we would return to the hotel room and review our notes. Jeff would get out his yellow legal-sized notepad and explain to us that based on the costs of running a mail-order business, it would be years, if ever, before we turned a profit. We all came to fear his yellow notepad and the bleak reality that always followed. Brad learned that outsourcing fulfillment may be the way to go and how this might help us reduce costs and make us more efficient. My head was swimming with information, and my eyes would pretty much glaze over at this point.

Diane was the only one who seemed energized by all she was learning. The numbers and formulas made sense to her, and she was actually having fun learning about circulation. Before long, we would all drop into bed for another sleepless night filled with snoring so we could start it over again the next morning.

Our First Consultant

By the third day of the convention, I was convinced we must be doing something wrong. We were losing money by the boatload and had to turn things around quickly. There had to be a piece of this mail-order puzzle we were missing. I had heard one of the industry gurus speak earlier that day and decided I was going to work up the nerve to go talk to him to see if he could point out what I was doing wrong.

I wish I could tell you I handled this with grace and professionalism, but the fact is I cornered him at lunch. I walked up to his table and blurted out my quandary. He was nice enough not to shoo me away. I think he took pity on me and asked me to sit down. I showed him the current issue of the catalog and told him in a nutshell what our response rate was and where we were at in terms of the growth of the company.

The consultant asked to see a few of the spreadsheets I kept waving around. After reviewing those, he looked even more puzzled than I was. He asked me where I got the data in these spreadsheets. I told him all the data came from our software, MOM. He then told me that either the data was wrong or we just didn't know our software well enough to pull the correct data or we were really onto something.

He could tell I didn't quite understand, so he explained that the results he was reviewing were indeed phenomenal. Phenomenal? How could the data be phenomenal if we were still losing money? I told him we had yet to make a dime, so we were clearly doing something wrong. I could tell he was trying not to laugh. Instead, he patiently explained that of course we weren't making any money, nor should we be expecting to for another three-to-five years. What? I must have missed that memo.

I thought it took the average new business about three years to turn a profit, and I really hadn't even planned on being average. Now he was telling me it was going to take what added up to be well over five years before we were operating in the black. He explained that the typical mail-order business doesn't make money for about five to seven years, and sometimes it can take as long as ten, depending on how much financing you have in place. The less money you have to start your business, the longer it will take to grow your business to a profitable size. Given our lack of startup capital, he explained, we could plan on it taking at least seven years before we started seeing any black ink on the books.

Well, that was certainly not the news I was expecting. The convention was full of the unexpected.

The bad news, we learned, was that losing money was normal; the good news was that we hadn't lost nearly as much as we should have by then. The consultant then offered to review our business in detail and make recommendations for us on how we should proceed, for a fee, of course. He was the first consultant we ever hired. Working with him was an education in the business that actually would have come in very handy *before* I started a catalog, but never having been one to read the directions, I got this bit of insight late in the game. But not too late.

After reviewing all of our data, the consultant was convinced there was something wrong with the data or the way we were getting it. He wanted to pull the information from our software himself so he could be sure it was correct. After reviewing all of the data he pulled himself, we got a fax saying, "You have got the tiger by the tail" and informing us that our results were even better, not worse, than we had thought. The consulting team scheduled a trip to Las Vegas to meet with us and review the numbers and the prospects for the future of Femail Creations. At the meeting, we reviewed a best, worst, and most likely case scenario. All of the scenarios seemed frightening to me – all of them required far more capital than we had. I felt a bit like I was standing in front of one of the slot machines in Vegas, knowing I had a winner, but all out of coins.

Hiring Diane

On the way home from the convention, Diane handed me a note to read on the plane. I laughed when I opened it and discovered a list of pros and cons for hiring her. Diane said she enjoyed the convention so much and felt like she had learned a lot, and she wanted me to hire her to oversee our circulation for the catalog. She knew that mixing family and business can be a challenge, and in Diane's classic outspoken way, she wanted to address that right up front, so she had made a list of all of the reasons I should and should not hire her.

Amazingly, Diane is so honest about herself that her con list was as long as her pro list. I have to say that after reading her lists, I agreed with her assessments – both good and bad – and decided to take the risk of hiring yet another family member. Diane was certainly smart enough to handle our circulation, and her knack for managing people in a call center would also come in handy. So Diane, who lives in Phoenix, started working for Femail Creations as our first telecommuting employee.

Working with Diane was always exciting. Her organizational style is, well, shall we say a bit different than mine. She seems to think laundry baskets and filing cabinets are interchangeable! I, on the other hand, like everything filed away where it should be. Diane's filing "system" was to simply try to keep paper – of any kind – in one place.

And that place most often happened to be a laundry basket. So whenever we needed a document or spreadsheet that she had, it practically required a search and rescue team.

Sleep Became a Memory

We continued to plug away at the business and miraculously continued to be able to pay all of our bills. Around every corner seemed to be a sign we were on the right track and should keep going. And keep going we did, around the clock! I worked hours that should not have been humanly possible. I was a woman on a mission. In an effort to make sure my kids still knew they had a mom and I didn't miss any of their important activities, I would skip sleep rather than miss a hockey game or track meet. If somebody was going to get shortchanged, it was going to be me, not my kids. Sleep became a memory, something I thought about a lot but rarely found the time to do.

The folks at the Cook Shop, a local pizza place, were on a first name basis with us. We lived on whatever could be delivered to the office. Brad, Nina, and Ethan hung right there with us, putting in insane hours. However, I look back on those days fondly. Even with all of the long hours, we had a lot of fun and laughed often. Maybe it was just delirium setting in from lack of sleep!

Weathering Growth

Brad had joined me in the steep learning curve of catalog production and started helping me produce the catalogs on the computer. We added more software, bought fancy printers, and learned as we went. Inevitably, whenever there was a tight deadline, the computer would crash or the printer would jam, keeping us there all night. On one such night, I ran home to shower, and when I got back to the office I found Brad asleep – on a dog bed. Apparently he was so tired he decided to lie down while the pages were printing out (which can take hours) and figured he might as well have something soft underneath him. He went back to the warehouse and grabbed one of the dog beds we sold at the time and curled up like a puppy and fell asleep. If only we had sold cameras too!

As the catalog kept growing, so did our staff and so did our volume of inventory. We seemed to fit in this office just fine most of the year, but when the holiday season arrived things got a little cozy, and the inventory started spilling out into every nook and cranny. We had products stacked everywhere from the conference room to the restroom. All of this required elaborate spreadsheets keeping track of where all of the overstock was. It was quite comical to search a spreadsheet for a certain item only to discover the location listed as "women's bathroom."

It seemed we were always buying another computer or another printer. We (okay, not so much "we" as Jeff) spent more time moving furniture than we care to remember. Every time we thought we had the office configuration figured out, something else would change or we would figure out a better layout, and the desks would move again. We also needed additional employees, and managing them all became yet another one of my full-time jobs.

Our First Foray into Outsourcing

We decided to look into outsourcing the call center. Our needs were clearly exceeding our software and human resource capabilities. We found a family-owned company in Wisconsin that seemed like a good fit and decided to make the leap. The changeover gave us a lot more physical space in the office and eliminated the need for twenty-four-hour staff. It was really liberating to know that we could actually close the office at night – not that we did it very often, but just knowing that we could gave me hope that someday I might even get some of my life back, or at least some sleep!

By this point, we were starting to amass what we affectionately called our computer graveyard. Computers and printers seemed to break faster than we could fix them and, as is sadly true with most technology, it's often cheaper to replace than repair. And so our pile of monitors, cables, printers, fax machines, copiers, keyboards, and hard drives grew and grew, but the upside was that we had our very own parts supply when we needed it.

In the fall of 1999, Brad delivered the sad news that he and Nina had decided to move back to Utah to be near Nina's family. Of course, I understood and told him how much I appreciated all of their hard work. I didn't want to lose two of my valuable employees, but really it was Ethan I was going to miss the most. He had spent the first months of his life with us, and I was going to miss having him attached to my hip while I worked. The day they left was hard on all of us.

Oy, We Need a Web Site, Too?

When I launched Femail Creations, the World Wide Web was just becoming part of our daily reality. More and more often, customers were asking if we had a Web site. And when we said no, the pressure started to mount to get one – and soon. More and more businesses, especially small businesses, were launching sites where their customers could browse and even shop online. It was a whole new world, and obviously a natural fit for a catalog company. But I was still pretty much a techno-peasant at that point. I was just figuring out how to use email and certainly hadn't planned on having a Web site. Not only was I not on the information superhighway, I hadn't even found the on-ramp!

Eventually we had so many requests for a Web site, that we knew we had to do something. Once again, I turned to my brother Brian for his technical expertise, and pretty soon we were able to launch our site. At first (silly us) we thought of it as just another avenue for orders. Our customers had other ideas. They wanted information, the history of Femail Creations, pictures of the staff, and more. Pretty soon we had created a dynamic online community for women at www.femailcreations.com, all thanks to great ideas and suggestions from our customers.

Learning the Circulation Ropes

With fulfillment finally more stable, we could focus on other areas of the business and get back our growth plan. Next up was circulation. Our circulation needs were increasing as the size of Femail Creations increased. My sister Diane had been handling that area for the last few years and she decided she was in over her head and needed to step aside. Love that Diane – she even knew the perfect person to take over. She had met Steven Lett at one of the catalog conventions and thought highly of him. He had over twenty-five years experience in the cataloging industry and certainly understood the science of circulation better than we did. I didn't want to lose my working relationship with Diane – working together had always been such an adventure – but I knew she was right and respected her for recognizing her limits and step-ping aside. After two wonderful years, Diane's telecom-muting days came to an end and Steve and his team took over.

From then on, Diane's role at Femail Creations became that of chief sounding board. We talk often, and she can always be counted on to give me a shoulder to lean on and a safe place to vent my frustrations. Best of all, she helps me keep my sense of humor during the trying times.

Outsourcing, Part Two

The holidays were just around the corner when disaster struck in the form of a one-day sale. We thought we had covered all of our bases, and we had; unfortunately, our outsourced call center had not. They had ignored our projections and on the day of the sale had seriously under-staffed the call center, leaving thousands of customers with a busy signal. To add insult to injury, they had also failed to upload the current inventory file, so the cus-tomers who did manage to get through were being sold inventory we no longer had! It was a nightmare. A bad dream that ultimately ended up in a lawsuit. As painful as that experience was, I actually learned a lot. One of the main things I learned is that even if you prevail in a law-suit, as we did, the only ones who really win are the lawyers.

After that ugly experience, we had no choice but to find a new call center. In an effort to avoid communica-tion problems between the call center and the warehouse, we decided to find a place that could accommodate both. We thought we'd found such a place with another small, family-run company in Colorado. What a bumpy road that was! This time we just had a real clash of styles. Apparently, the owner there really wanted to be my best friend. When I declined an offer to spend a weekend at a spa with her, she pretty much flipped out and became unreasonable to deal with on any level. Frankly, I wasn't looking for new friends; I just wanted a company that I could count on for good service. At the end of a very long year, they sold the business to another company and we ended up having to relocate our fulfillment again.

They'd hardly given us any notice about the sale, so we had very little time to find a new fulfillment house. We decided to have Mountain West, the call center that was already handling our overflow volume, start handling our calls full-time since they were familiar with the cata-log and our products. They were great to work with and began handling all our calls. Now we just needed to find a warehouse to ship our orders.

In our rush to find one we ended up with a fulfillment company in Utah that knew far less about fulfillment than we did! The systems they professed to have were actually still in the developmental stage, and they were chroni-cally understaffed and mismanaged. Within a few weeks, I knew we'd made a colossal mistake and that if we didn't get out of there, they would put us out of business. So we took a deep breath and faced our fourth fulfillment move in two years.

We found a company in Ohio that could run both the warehouse and the call center. We went back to the old arrangement, with our current call center handling our nighttime and overflow calls and our new call center handling the day shift. This proved to be a win-win situation for all three companies.

To say that running a business is an adventure is a gross understatement. Years ago, I ripped this page from my daily calendar and tacked it up where I can always see it.

> We can never see the path of our life if we are too busy focusing on the pebbles under our feet. There are times when we have to stop and look for vistas.

I have learned that when disaster strikes – and it will – you just have to keep moving, keep your sense of humor, and keep looking for vistas.

facing our fears

4

When I dare to be powerful –
to use my strength in the service of my vision –
then it becomes less and less important
whether or not I am afraid.

— AUDRE LORDE

I USED TO THINK THAT THERE WERE SOME PEOPLE, some other breed of people, who simply did not get scared. I thought they tackled things in life head-on without blinking. I wanted to be one of those people. But what I have discovered over the years is that there is no such breed. Courageous people aren't unafraid; they just do it anyway.

One of my teachers of this life lesson was a woman I knew who was a competitive athlete. I had always been in awe of women like her, who dared to travel to distant lands, run across deserts, climb mountains, or kayak down the world's fiercest rivers. As she described an upcoming one-hundred-mile adventure run and the grueling days ahead, I told her I honestly didn't think I would have the guts, even if I did have the athletic ability. Her response shocked me. She said, "Oh, I'm terrified, but I do it anyway."

In that spirit, many summers ago I talked my brother Brad into taking me and my friend and sister-in-law Julie on a backpacking expedition. We wanted to commune with nature, I said, to face our fears and expand our comfort zones. Brad is a woodsy kind of guy and was in great shape at the time (no offense little brother, but we were all in better shape back then). He had survived the military's basic training and come out with a set of dress blues, so we figured he was just the guy for the job. If he could survive basic training, he could easily survive us for three days!

Julie and I set out to gather all of the gear we would need. We treated ourselves to new backpacks, sleeping bags, a water purifier, and the tiniest stove I have ever seen. I must have tried on one hundred pairs of hiking boots looking for a pair that wouldn't give me blisters. My feet are known for being high maintenance. (I personally consider them low maintenance; after all, they prefer to be bare – how much more low maintenance can they be?) Let's just say if blisters were a commodity, I would be rich! My tootsies blister at the mere sight of shoes, so you can imagine how they felt about hiking boots.

We met up with Brad at the mouth of Zion National Park. The towering red rocks and mountains of stone were breathtaking. As we drove up the canyon, Brad pointed to a peak far off in the distance and told us we were going to climb to the top. All I can tell you now is that it was a good thing we thought he was joking! Had we known he was serious we would never have left the parking lot.

We parked in the grotto and piled up our gear. When Brad saw just how big our pile was, he got this look on his face that told me we had perhaps overpacked just a bit. All he said, however, was "bring whatever you want to carry." That word "carry" really carried a lot of weight – no pun intended. Okay, maybe I didn't need that pound of red licorice after all. Now, I'm all for gender equality, but I confess, I was awfully glad my brother offered to carry most of the water (did you know that water weighs about eight pounds a gallon?)!

We headed up the mountain – and I do mean *up*. Those switchbacks gave new meaning to the word *steep*. It didn't take long for me to realize that I would not only be needing first aid for my blisters, but perhaps oxygen, too! I was sucking some serious air! After a few miles, the day hikers thinned out and it was just our party of three panting our way up the West Rim.

For a while, the incredible views kept my mind off the heavy pack strapped to my back. When the sun started to set, Brad picked up the pace in an effort to get us to the only spot on the mountain flat enough to pitch our tent for the night. I like to think it was the fact that we got off to a late start rather than that Julie and I couldn't keep up that prevented us from reaching our campsite that night. Whatever the case may have been, we ended up sleeping – I use the term loosely – on a slab of granite with a serious slope.

When the sun came up, we got a good look at our makeshift campsite and had a good laugh. We were practically sliding off the mountain. We wanted to get an early start so as not to get caught in the dark again, so we had a quick breakfast and started packing up our gear. It was then that I got to experience the joy of putting my feet back into those hiking boots. Ouch! And ouch, again and again, with each step from then on. I had to keep reminding myself that we had *asked* him to take us on this journey. We were the ones who wanted to "face our fears and expand our comfort zones."

Indeed, when our backpacking trip was over and we hiked those last few steps and dropped our packs, it didn't feel as much like the weight of the world had been lifted from our tired shoulders as that our worlds had expanded to include this new experience. The trip *was* a real growing experience, and just a few months after our maiden backpacking quest, Julie and I went on our own backpacking adventure, without our fearless leader. A major achievement, I must say.

I can tell you this, once you expand your comfort zone it will just keep growing, and so will you! What is it that your heart longs to try but maybe you have been afraid to take the leap? Face your fear and step out on that limb. There is no time like the present! As we expand our comfort zones, we expand our possibilities.

Sometimes life serves up the opportunities to grow and expand our comfort zones, and sometimes we have to create the opportunities for ourselves. I was so proud of my little sister Jennifer when she found the courage to pack up her life, leaving her friends and a job she loved behind to move thousands of miles away and go back to school to become a midwife. Facing the fear of leaving the known for the unknown can be the biggest leap of all.

Fear

Finding and following your passion can be scary. Throughout much of my journey I have been afraid. I was afraid to say out loud what I wanted to do. I was afraid my family would suffer because of my decision to start my own business. I was afraid we would lose our house because of the debt we had amassed to finance the business. I feared not being able to find the stamina to see this thing through. But I continue to put one fearful foot forward and take it a step at a time. I truly have learned that courage comes in all shapes and sizes and often comes with a healthy dose of fear. As Louisa May Alcott says, "I am not afraid of storms, for I'm learning to sail my ship."

Money, Money, Money

One of the biggest, scariest risks I ever took was getting a Small Business Administration loan to fund my mission and grow Femail Creations. I have always felt that the obstacles that can be overcome by hard work are the easy ones. It is the challenges that hard work alone can't fix that scare me the most. Financing was definitely one of those challenges. For most of its run, Femail Creations has been funded on a hope and a prayer. After three years, it became painfully clear that no matter how many times I mortgaged my house and begged and borrowed, we still needed to find a large sum of capital to keep going. So I reluctantly turned to my bank. I did not want to take on any more debt, but the reality was that the mail-order industry is a very capital-intensive business and we simply were in over our heads.

Our then current bank offered SBA loans, so I figured I'd contact them first. We had been with them for several years, and I happened to know the president from my days of volunteer work. I called her up one day and explained why I felt an SBA loan was the best route for the business to take. She agreed and directed me to her senior loan officer. I gave him a call and set up an appointment for the following week. He told me I would need to provide stacks of financial information prior to our meeting. I gathered everything on the list and sent it to him.

I spent days reviewing the financials and our business outline so I would be ready. The morning of the appointment, the loan officer called to make sure my husband would be coming with me to the meeting. I hadn't planned on bringing Jeff, but he did bank there as well and was friendly with all of the staff, so I figured they were just being gracious about inviting him along. I checked with my husband to see if he could join us. He was free, so we decided to go to the appointment and then have lunch together afterwards.

When we arrived at the bank, we were greeted by a woman I had done banking business with before. She said she would be sitting in on the meeting as well. I was so relieved, thinking I might get to work with her on the loan. She explained that she didn't handle SBA loans or loans of this size but had been asked to join the meeting because she was familiar with my business.

We were ushered into a large conference room with a huge table and about a dozen chairs. I took a chair and sat down, and Jeff sat next to me on the right. The woman I knew sat on my left, and the loan officer sat across the table from all of us. I pulled out all of my spreadsheets and company information as well as a copy of the current catalog, but before I could even begin to review the numbers, the loan officer leaned across the table and looked directly at my husband. He said that he didn't want to waste anybody's time so he was going to get right to the point. He then told Jeff that his wife needed a new hobby, that selling crafts through a catalog was a bad idea, and that he didn't understand who would want to buy this rubbish or who we would market it to.

My husband and I were shocked. Jeff grabbed my arm, I think he was afraid of what my response might be – that is, that I would lunge across the table. Even the woman from the bank seemed stunned. It was one of the few times in my life when I was left speechless.

Jeff leaned in and said, jaw clenched, "I am not sure what you mean. My wife is running a business, not a hobby. And apparently a lot of people want to buy these items, because her sales were over $3 million last year. Is that what you call a hobby?"

To which the man replied, "It may well have millions of dollars in sales, but this is nothing more than an expensive hobby. I suggest you tell your wife to find another way to spend her time before she loses all of your money."

I could not believe what I was hearing. We were at a bank, in what I thought was a professional meeting, in what I thought was the 1990s. How could this be happening?

At that point, Jeff stood up. He said, "It is clear to me that you are not taking this business seriously, so I have to assume you don't take our money very seriously either, and if that is the case we will be moving our funds and banking business – for both companies – elsewhere." We gathered our things and walked out.

When I got back to the office that afternoon, I called my accountant, who also happened to be a family friend, and told him what had happened at the bank. He couldn't believe it either and suggested that I at least call the bank president, let her know what her employee said, and give her a chance to straighten things out. I called immediately and let her know how offended I'd been. I also suggested that she talk to the other woman in the room to confirm my version of events. She promised to do that and call me back.

That was a waste of time! When she called back all she had to say was that she had worked with this man for many years and had to trust his judgment. If he felt that this business was a lost cause, she had to take him at his word. She said she didn't necessarily agree with the way he delivered his verdict, but that she had to trust his business sense. This was one tough woman, who had fought hard to get where she was, and I couldn't believe she was willing to allow this kind of sexist behavior in her bank.

I confirmed that we would be moving all of our money out of her bank. At the time that consisted of our personal accounts, the business accounts for both companies, and the merchant accounts for our credit card services for the catalog, which made a lot of money for the bank.

I then called my accountant again and asked him if he could recommend another bank. He suggested First Security bank. I called that day and set up an appointment with their SBA loan officer, Colletta. She asked to see the same financials and business outlines that I had already prepared, so we were able to meet the following day. Colletta thought the catalog had real potential and recommended to the bank that they proceed with the SBA loan application.

Let me tell you, filling out an SBA loan application is no small feat. Once again, my sister Diane came to the rescue.

Her son is handicapped, so she has spent his lifetime filling out mountains of government paperwork for his care. I knew she would know where to start. Diane helped me prepare all the forms and fill out all the documents for my next round of meetings. It was at those meetings that I learned I needed a business plan – a *real* business plan. What did I do? I called Diane, of course, and said, "Have I got a project for you!" Always willing to help, Diane jumped on board to help me create and write our first formal business plan – after three years in business.

Once the business plan was submitted, Colletta said I would have to meet with Bruce. From what I understood, he was the guy who would make or break the deal. I was going to be darn sure I was prepared for that meeting. After my first experience with the top dog at my last bank, I was more than nervous about how this meeting would go. Everyone who knew Bruce told me he was a real numbers guy, and I had better know my facts and figures. I studied those spreadsheets front to back and sideways for a week to get ready for my meeting with Bruce. There wasn't a fact about the industry or the current position of my company that I couldn't answer. I was ready. Scared but ready.

The day for the big meeting came, and Bruce arrived at my office to tour our facility and review my final application. Just to add to my nerves, Bruce had quite a presence! He was over six feet tall and looked like he was with the NBA, not the SBA! His stature did nothing to calm my nerves.

We began the meeting by reviewing the numbers. We discussed our current sales figures, and I thoroughly explained why it takes so long to break even in this odd business. I explained how costly it is to prospect in order to build what is known in the industry as a "house file." Once a catalog's house file is large enough, it begins to support the business. But until it reaches that size, you must do a lot of expensive prospecting for new customers. It takes a typical catalog about five to seven years to get to that point. It can happen faster if you have a lot of capital and can aggressively prospect to build the business. Or it can take ten years if you bootstrap the operation.

Bruce listened patiently as I explained the data and nature of the mail-order industry. He had plenty of questions, and I had plenty of answers. He seemed satisfied with all of my answers, and I was relieved that it seemed like we were about to wrap up the meeting. Bruce said he felt confident that I would work hard to see the catalog succeed, but he did have one reservation before he could give this loan his approval. The charity work we did. Bruce said he didn't see how in good conscious he could sign off on a loan for a company that had yet to make money and featured a charity in every issue of the catalog. He said he applauded my compassion and thought it would be a great thing to bring back into the catalog once we were making money. But, he said, giving away money when you aren't making any lacked business sense and financial responsibility.

I was crushed. I knew it would mean not getting the loan, but I simply would not compromise on this issue. It didn't sound like Bruce could either. I understood his concern from a financial standpoint, but I had started the catalog in order to make a difference and I wasn't about to abandon that mission. As far as I was concerned, giving back was the heart and soul of Femail Creations.

At this point, I figured I would face my fear of not getting the loan and take the risk and let Bruce know just how passionate I was about making a difference. I took a deep breath and looked Bruce in the eye and said, "Bruce, I will understand if you can't give me this loan, and I hope you will understand why I can't take the charity out of the catalog." Bruce was silent for a while and then shook his head. I knew it was over.

Instead, this courageous man looked up and said, "I am going to give you this loan. I know one thing for sure: If this business doesn't succeed, it won't be because of lack of hard work or passion on your part. You've got guts, and if anyone can do this, you can." He shook my hand and left.

Colletta called that afternoon to tell me that Bruce had signed off on the loan. I was elated! Rumor had it that Bruce was amazed that I had dared to stand my ground on the charity even though my loan was on the line. Sometimes chutzpah pays off! Not only did I get the loan, but I got it by facing my fears and without compromising what I believed in. It restored my hope in people and in what I was doing.

A little over a year later, I received the Small Business Administration's Business Person of the Year award. When I spoke at the awards luncheon, I thanked Bruce and Colletta and the team at our new bank for believing in Femail Creations. As I looked out over the audience, I saw a familiar face at the table right in front of the podium – the president of the first bank that had turned me down in such a harsh way. After the luncheon, she graciously congratulated me on my award and wished me continued success.

Now we had the cash we needed to make it through the next few years – until it was time to mortgage the house again. But having that loan payment to make each month was another opportunity to face my fears. Taking on that much debt was scary, and many days it still is, so I just take a deep breath and pretend there are fewer zeroes than there really are on my SBA loan amount. Anais Nin once wrote, "Life shrinks or expands in proportion to one's courage." Apparently so do SBA loans.

Writing this book was another huge step outside of my comfort zone. Many times during this process, I questioned why I agreed to do it. My internal critics would come to life and give me a thousand reasons why I shouldn't and couldn't. After an especially rough few days with what one might affectionately call "writer's block," I took Jeff and my son, Bridger, to dinner at Carlos, my favorite Mexican restaurant. I adore the chef as much as I adore his cooking. I was in need of some comfort and some inspiration. I knew Carlos and his tacos would provide just the comfort food I was looking for, and I was counting on his margaritas to provide the inspiration.

Jeff and Bridger were sitting across from me at the table as I shared my fears and concerns that maybe I didn't have it in me to finish this book while also still trying to run a business and finish the catalog production on the next issue. It was Bridger who chimed in first, saying, "Mom, you can do it. You always do it. Look at how many things you have accomplished that you didn't think you could. You should tell other women about Femail Creations and maybe it will inspire them to follow their dreams. You always tell me I can do anything. Well, so can you." Out of the mouth of babes . . .

It was my hope of inspiring other women – and a little encouragement from my then thirteen-year-old son – that gave me the courage to be afraid – and to keep going anyway.

attempting the
impossible

5

*Only she who attempts the absurd can achieve
the impossible.*   — ROBIN MORGAN

ACCORDING TO SCIENTISTS AND THE LAWS
of aerodynamics, honeybees shouldn't be able to
fly, and according to my accountant, Femail Creations
shouldn't still be in business. The fact that Female Creations is still kicking is a testament to the fact that the
impossible is possible. The enormous obstacles Female
Creations has had to overcome seem impossible even to
the most optimistic among us. I guess having always been
a glass-half-full kind of gal has come in handy!

One day years ago, a letter from a customer came at
just the perfect moment. It was a particularly trying time,
business wise, and I needed some sign that I was not crazy
to hang in there. As I was packing up one evening, I
decided to sit down and read my mail. Good thing, too!
A customer named Liz had written me a little note to let
me know how much she loved Femail Creations and

looked forward to each and every issue of the catalog. She explained that she was living on a limited income and couldn't shop as often as she would like, but she wanted me to know just how much Femail Creations meant to her. She included $2 in the envelope, four quarters and a dollar bill, along with the explanation that she wanted me to put this toward the next catalog to make sure there was one. I can't tell you how touched I was.

With tears streaming down my face, I read her note over and over again. I just couldn't believe that a complete stranger would make a gesture like that. I actually have that very note and that very money still hanging up on a bulletin board in my office to remind me that the work I do does matter.

I shared the story of Liz's letter with my friend Cathy Conheim, founder of the Real Women's Project, an organization dedicated to helping women realize and celebrate their inherent beauty, dignity, and capacity for transformation. Cathy, too, was moved by the spirit of the letter and the amazing way Femail Creations touches our customers. I shared with Cathy how difficult it was to be constantly stressed by lack of funding. Cathy told me she thought I should share that truth with our customers and ask them to do just what Liz had done.

At first, I thought the idea was crazy. Why would our customers be willing to send in money to help a struggling business? Cathy reminded me that they too cared about this business and challenged me to at least try. It was true. We were seriously strapped for cash, but more importantly, I wanted to share with our Femail family how significant *they* were to the success of the catalog. I wanted them to see the power of their shopping dollars and the difference they could make. And I needed to know if what I was doing mattered. I wanted their vote of confidence and their encouragement that we were on the right track.

So, with as much courage as I could muster, I sent out an email to my whole customer list, sharing the story of receiving Liz's note and gift and the impact it had had on me. Within the week, we started receiving letters with coins and dollar bills inside – hundreds of them. By daring to break all the business rules and asking our customers for financial help, we raised over three thousand dollars. Not a fortune by business standards – the money only helped pay a small portion of the postage on the next mailing of the catalog – but the feedback and support from these letters was priceless and gave me the courage and inspiration to go on.

They don't teach you that kind of thing in business school! And yet more times than I can count, it was the positive feedback from customers and artists that kept me going when things felt impossible. I think it's a she thing. Women just function best in community, don't you think? To this day whenever doubt creeps in or I start to feel overwhelmed at the challenge of running a business, I read my mail and find inspiration all over again.

Lisa and the Purple School

I confess I have something of a history of attempting the impossible. One of my kids' favorite stories about their crazy mom always attempting the impossible goes back to when my daughter was starting second grade and a new elementary school was being built practically across the street. Harlie was so excited about the prospect of getting to walk to school like all the other big kids. My own enthusiasm waned, however, when I discovered that the school was going to be painted purple! As a volunteer at the school, I was meeting with the principal when he mentioned the school colors. Not that I don't enjoy the color purple – I love the color purple – as a movie, just not as a school.

I sprang into action. I called my good friend Kris, who was then president of the Parent-Teacher Organization and told her the school was about to get a purple paint job. I was vice president in charge of fund raising for the PTO at the time and spoke with Kris almost daily. She wasn't exactly happy about the color either.

I happened to know the general contractor on the project, so I just walked over to his construction trailer to have a chat. In between chuckles, Keith explained that the color for all the schools is decided at the district level months if not years in advance of the job. He said, "If you think you can do anything about the color of a school, you've obviously never experienced the joys of government bureaucracy."

I left the trailer ready for the challenge. I called Kris and told her we were going to have to take this to the district level to get anything done. We went right to the principal of the new school and told him we wanted the school painted a different color. He thought we were nuts, but he'd also worked with us long enough to know that we weren't going to take no for an answer. He said he frankly didn't care what color his school was, but if it mattered so much to us, we should take it to the district.

The next day, Kris and I showed up at the district offices and asked to speak to somebody about the color of our elementary school. We could hear the laughter and whispers coming from the back room, but when they realized we weren't going away one of the senior staff members came out to speak with us. He said, "Ladies, changing the color of the school at this point is impossible; frankly, it's a request we just can't even entertain." And then he gave us the go-away-before-I-call-security look.

Two such stubborn and determined women weren't about to be told no. I am telling you, staying home fulltime made me do some crazy things to keep my spirit alive and my brain from turning to mush. I am sure other mothers came up with better ways, but this was mine.

I won't bore you with the tale of all the antics we tried, but my guess is that the district people finally got so sick of seeing us (and probably started worrying what other battles we might fight!) that they not only let us pick the paint color but the furniture and the carpeting too! You should have seen the look on that contractor's face when we walked back into his trailer to tell him the news! What can I say? Never mess with a woman on a mission! I drive by that school every day, and it still makes me smile to think that we did the "impossible."

When you're convinced that you're on the right track, don't take no for an answer. Dare to dream the impossible, and then follow through. Your dreams can come true.

stepping stone

Sometimes we just need a shove in the right direction to see the impossible as possible. When I asked Amy Peters, a dear friend and incredible entrepreneur, about how she found the courage to start her own jewelry company she said:

> Years ago before I started my business, I was working in a craft gallery, watching everyone else making and selling wonderful work, and I was too afraid to take the leap. One day a successful artist who I admired told me something that his art professor had told him in college. His professor had always said, "If you haven't used your art to make a living five years after graduating from art school, you never will." It had been four years and six months for me, and I had been seriously dragging my feet about selling my jewelry designs. What ifs were keeping me from doing it. *What if I can't pay off my student loans with the money I make . . . if there is any money at all? What if I spend a lot of time making my art and I can't sell it?* I was wallowing in negativity and self-doubt. But the comment scared me to death. If I didn't turn my lifelong hobby into a career now, I doubted that I ever would.
>
> I realized that my fear of being on my deathbed and regretting the fact that I didn't ever try was much worse than the possibility of failing at something. So I took the leap. I rented a nine-by-fifteen-foot shed with a dirt floor and no running water, filed my business paperwork, and started to create designs to show the owners of the gallery where I worked.
>
> About a month later I had a collection that I felt was good enough to show. I remember being scared to death the day I brought the designs into the store. One of the owners was known for laughing at art that

wasn't up to her quality standards. But I just put all my designs out in front of her, and she loved each and every one of them and took them all to sell in the store. And they sold one by one. I went on to create more and more work for the gallery and then expanded to sell to other stores.

I still remember saying that I'd feel like I'd made it once I had five stores selling my work. Eight years later and with over 700 stores and national catalogs now selling my work, I have never regretted one minute of taking that initial leap. It has been a roller coaster ride of ups and downs, but it has been so worth it. I now spend a little bit of each day mentoring other emerging artists and encouraging them to follow their hearts and dreams.

Building My Dream House

Whenever something starts to feel really impossible I like to remind myself of times when the impossible happened – whether for me or for somebody else. It never hurts to have a reminder that miracles *do* happen. I actually reside in one.

I always knew I wanted to build my own house and constantly kept my eye out for a lot to build on. When a new development across the street started selling lots, I picked the one I wanted and drove by it frequently. Never mind the fact we couldn't afford this piece of land; this is the one I had my heart set on. I just *knew* this was my future address. I had such certainly about it that I didn't really worry too much about the fact that we couldn't afford it. I just kept saving every dime I could. At that point, my husband had only recently started his own construction company, and things were beyond tight. We never ate out or went to the movies or traveled or did anything that might slow down our savings.

After two years of watching this corner lot, I decided it was finally time to go see what the current price was. Imagine my shock when the developer told me the lot had already been sold over a year ago. How dare somebody buy *my* lot? It was only a few days later that I learned that the people who had bought the lot were actually friends of ours, and we soon found out that they had already drawn up house plans and were scheduled to break ground in a few months. However, I was still convinced that this was where I was supposed to live, so I was really confused. How was I going to build there if they were?

The next time I saw our friends I told them they had bought *my* lot. I am sure they thought I was nuts, but I told them they really should start looking for a different piece of land. I just *knew* something would work out, and for once, I patiently waited as the answer unfolded. Many months later it did. It turned out that our friends decided to build a cabin instead of a new home, and they were going to sell the lot after all. After two years of waiting, we were finally in a position to buy the land.

The only way we could afford to build on the lot was if I subcontracted out the house myself rather than hire a general contractor – not something I would recommend for the faint of heart. Construction was still a man's world, and they weren't too thrilled to see me coming. Building that house myself was a huge life lesson in trusting your gut and not being afraid of being "where you don't belong." I am proud to say we finished the project on our meager budget and ahead of schedule. Our address has proven to be a lesson in miracles. The tenacity it took to build our home is the same tenacity it took to start a business. Years later when I started the catalog, I found myself drawing on that experience and remembering that miracles do happen. And it is a good thing I did build that house – it would be the same house, unbeknownst to me, that I would be mortgaging over and over again to finance Femail Creations.

Miracles do happen, but they take a lot of miraculous hard work!

 stepping stone

Kelly Stone and Planet Hope

Kelly Stone knows all about overcoming the odds and achieving the impossible. When Kelly was only twenty-nine, she had a great job and a wonderful future ahead of her. She just didn't realize how much that future was about to change. Leaving work one evening as the director of marketing for a large medical firm, she slipped and fell down thirteen stairs. The accident left her in a wheelchair and facing many operations and complications. After many months of a downward spiral, Kelly was out of work, out of money, and out of hope. It was her sister, the actress Sharon Stone, who pulled her out of bed and took her to a home for teenage girls. That day Kelly stopped thinking about her own problems and started focusing on others.

She started volunteering on crutches and never stopped. With Sharon's help, Kelly went on to found Planet Hope, a foundation to help homeless women and children. As Kelly puts it, "after the accident I realized I needed to help people who were hopeless." Each summer, Planet Hope organizes Camp Hope for homeless children and their mothers. My daughter, Harlie, had the privilege of volunteering at Camp Hope this summer and said the experience changed her life. Harlie came home filled with touching stories about the incredible women and children she met and admiration for Kelly for having had the courage to create such a wonderful foundation that helps so many.

I came to know Kelly when we featured Planet Hope in the catalog as one of our Making a Difference charities. Kelly told me: "the response I get from Femail Creations customers moves me every day." When she asked if her Hollywood marketing agency could represent us, she didn't give up until I said yes.

She said that we were just the kind of "company with heart" that she wanted to work with.

Kelly's advice to other women who want to attempt the impossible? "Follow every day with a positive spirit. Love yourself first and go after every dream."

merchandising with heart and soul

6

Creations, whether they are children, poems, or organizations, take on a life of their own.

— STARHAWK

Gifts of the Heart and Soul

One of my central focuses at Femail Creations is and always has been to find creations crafted with heart and soul. I don't simply want to sell "product"; I want to offer inspiring gifts that are really meaningful for the recipient – even, or perhaps especially, if that gift happens to be for yourself!

For the first year or two, I simply hunted and gathered near home. Then one day, one of the artists I tracked down asked me if I was going to the San Francisco Gift Show. Gift show? What's a gift show? I had no idea. As luck had it, I was planning to be in the Bay Area that weekend anyway to visit my friend, the author and artist SARK. She was having a slumber party, and I didn't want to miss it!

Hundreds of SARK fans converged at the Hotel Monaco wearing our Karen Neuburger pajamas to hear SARK speak and the Australian band the Velvet Janes play. It was a fabulous evening!

Meeting Karen Neuburger was also a treat. I think she's a brilliant businesswoman! Karen Neuburger – founder, president, and design director of Karen Neuburger Sleepwear – created her namesake company shortly after the birth of her second child and, ironically, just as she was planning to retire. A respected sportswear designer, she was continually looking for comfortable, attractive loungewear and discovered that nothing was available. "It's a well-kept secret that women have an all-day love affair with their sleepwear," explains Neuburger, who confesses to wearing her favorite "boyfriend pajamas" at any time of the day or night. "Realizing that, I was able to give sleepwear many sportswear features, making them even more wearable. It's a lifestyle choice and a passion for comfort." When I asked her for advice, she told me that women often think too small when it comes to business and encouraged me to think bigger!

My First Gift Show

With my creative juices flowing, I headed off to my first-ever gift show. There are many gift shows around the country each year. No matter what industry you are in, there is probably a trade show specializing in products and services for your business. The huge Moscone Convention center was filled with aisle after aisle of wholesale vendors selling everything from jewelry to clothing to furniture to food. Most of the buyers there were from stores and would actually be placing orders for inventory at the gift show; As a catalog, we just select samples for consideration to include in upcoming issues of Femail Creations. In the past, we'd always found our artists (or had them find us) through word of mouth. The idea of having so many vendors all in one place was like a dream come true.

But what I quickly discovered was that finding artists who still handcraft their work was going to be like finding a needle in a haystack. Now that I've been to dozens and dozens of shows, I know that most of the products at gift shows are imported and mass-produced, but this was the first eye-opener. We did find a special section devoted to handcrafted art, and that's where we did our business. It turns out that most shows have a section like that, and that's where we always head first.

Doing Business with Heart

You are probably aware that most imported merchandise is made in heartbreaking conditions. It's because we don't want to support bad labor practices that Femail Creations has always focused on supporting artisans who handcraft their work here in America. But this has been a huge challenge on many fronts. There simply aren't as many artists doing that kind of work as there used to be, as more and more companies choose the more lucrative route of importing mass-produced merchandise from overseas. Not only are the artisans hard to find, but competing financially with the importers has proven to be one of our greatest obstacles.

It can be hard for a customer to understand why she should buy a necklace from our catalog for thirty-nine dollars when she can find a similar one at the mall for fifteen.

The fact is the store at the mall most likely bought its necklace from China for about a fourth (or less!) of the retail price, whereas we pay twenty dollars for our thirty-nine-dollar necklace and it was crafted by hand here in America. We try to educate our customers about these issues through our catalogs – we explain that an item that is hand-fabricated, sculpted, etched, or embellished and individually created is going to cost more than one that is made by a machine or in a sweatshop. They realize that with us their dollars are making a real difference – and that matters.

What Sustains Me

One of our customers wrote to tell us about her two boys, both in their early twenties and both in the military. After the terrorist attacks on September 11th, both sons were scheduled to be sent off in service. The woman purchased two of the handcrafted necklaces from our catalog that said, "I love you this much," and gave one to each of her boys that year for Christmas. She wrote to tell me just how touched her boys were and thanked me for doing the work I do.

I get so many letters and emails like this, and it's often what keeps me going. Recently I received a letter that broke and healed my heart at the same time. Let me share a bit of it with you.

> I'd like to thank you for the most precious possession I currently have as a result of your website and magazine. This is a true story.
>
> In October of 2002, my childhood best friend of twenty-two years, Melissa Ann Melson, called to tell me that she had found the perfect birthday present for

me. She was so excited that she couldn't decide whether to send it to my home, or bait me with the gift to entice me to visit her new house! Birthday presents, friendship, and water sports on the canal in Key West; we made a tentative plan to spend Thanksgiving together.

On November 9, while walking her dog, Melissa slipped on some coral in a shallow part of the water and was knocked unconscious and drowned. The Stock Island Canal took her life.

A few days later, I received my birthday gift in the mail. It was the heart-shaped plaque from your catalog that reads: "Never forget to kiss each other goodnight."

The last earthly tangible item that I have to remember Melissa by is this plaque that she was so excited to give me. I am grateful and speechless. She knew I would love it, and I do!

Her memorial service was beautiful with twenty-five butterflies released and tons of tealight candles lit at sunset floating down the canal. Melissa always wore a smile on her lips and on her heart, and at her service one of her friends said that they would miss their MacGuyver girl! She could change a tire, and maintain her sweet femininity at the same time.

I just wanted you to know about this. This art shed light on her life, and will continue to remind me of the excitement and love of our friendship.

Having a customer take the time to share such a personal and heartfelt story with me touched me deeply.

Another customer recently wrote to me with this incredible account. It gives me goose bumps every time I share this story.

I work with a woman who has kept up a close relationship with her college roommates for decades. One of them purchased your "protect this woman" bracelet for each in their group. One of the women in the group is a nurse at St. Vincent's hospital in NYC, the closest facility to the World Trade Center. When the disaster hit on 9-11, Mary and her friends were worried about their "sister"; no one had heard from her. Then, a news photo in a national publication showed a poignant photo of a nurse who had bent down behind to hug a distraught African American woman victim who was sitting on the curb outside the hospital. You couldn't see the nurse's face – just her signature red hair and her "protect this woman" bracelet. They knew she was safe.

Hearing from my customers is just one of the deeply rewarding aspects of meaningful work. There are many other rewards, too. I have to travel a lot for this business, but one of the most rewarding parts about going all around the country to shows is getting to meet the incredibly talented artists who make these wonderful handcrafted gifts. Sometimes when I don't think I can bear one more road trip, it is the anticipation of dinner with an artist I adore or of drinks with fellow business owners Coco and Tommy that gets me on the plane once again. I feel like our vendors are all part of the Femail Creations family. We are all working and learning together toward a common goal.

As Katherine Mansfield once said, "I am treating you as my friend, asking you to share my present minuses in the hope I can ask you to share my future pluses."

Knowing that the mission of Femail Creations matters

and makes a difference to our artists in the catalogs means a great deal to me. I recently received an email from Stacey, one of the artists in the catalog who took the time to write and share with me her gratitude.

> Lisa . . . I have been telling *everyone* about your catalog. I get an incredible feeling just looking through it. You have truly done so much to reach women and young girls of all ages. Just by helping or teaching them to revel in themselves and their "femail hood." I feel honored to be a part of Femail Creations and will continue to share your catalog and its contents with all my friends, customers and new acquaintances. You do things the way I would and treat people the way I like to, with dignity, respect and importance. Your Making a Difference outreach program makes you all the more special. Thank you again. You have inspired me and helped me to find within myself a wellspring of creativity. You are impacting more people than you know and for that I am grateful. Keep up the good work and keep the dream alive.

I also love finding a new item at a show and watching it evolve into a great seller, both because I love seeking out new merchandise and because I love to support the artists. Sending big purchase orders (and checks) to our artists still delights me.

Don't let me give you the wrong impression, I have certainly had my share of dogs – that is what we call a very poor selling item. (Much to my Airedale Zoë's dismay!) Probably my biggest dog to date has to be the popcorn and chocolate mint bath gel we tried to sell years ago. Emphasis on tried! My sister Cynthia and I were both sure this was going to be a real winner. The popcorn lotion smelled so good, and we just knew women everywhere were going to love the chocolate mint bath gel.

And we were not alone. The vendor's booth was jammed full of people falling over themselves to get a sample. That big hit in the booth just didn't translate at all into print. Maybe it was the fact that it was lunchtime and we were starving when we first saw the products, or maybe they would have sold better in a store where you could smell it – or maybe not! Maybe people just want to eat popcorn, not smell like it. Whatever the reason, it was a huge flop, and we ended up giving thousands of tubes and bottles away to charity.

Amy Peters, one of the artists in Femail Creations, shared these thoughts about her own experiences shopping at Femail Creations.

> I had been working with Femail Creations for about two years when a dear friend of mine called to tell me that she had a rare condition that required immediate brain surgery. She explained that there was a chance she wouldn't make it through the operation. I was shocked and scared for her and I didn't have a clue as to what I could say or do to help her through this . . . My goodness, it was brain surgery after all . . . What could I possibly do to help. I thought immediately about Femail Creations. I flipped through the pages looking for something, anything that would express to her how much I was pulling for her.
>
> I picked out a pair of Footzenwarmer fleece booties, a lavender pillow with the word *Hope* written on it and the book entitled *Women of Courage*. And I placed an

order to be delivered immediately. After her successful surgery and full recovery she told me that she had spent the night before the operation reading *Women of Courage*, the Footzenwarmers on her feet and the Hope pillow on her chest. She relayed her gratitude for helping her through the most stressful evening of her entire life. Femail Creations makes it possible to find just the right items for any occasion.

I've always felt that products can be more than just products and business doesn't always have to be just about business. That's why I do this. Artist Lori Rodgers said:

> Femail Creations came to me at a time in my life where I was flailing. You bought and sold all my stuff and I was revived! I thought I was a failure because I was financially busted but working with you lifted my spirit and now I am a maniac again! I love making new things to sell to the most wonderful catalog I know. I have never had so much personal feedback as I do from the Femail Creations customers. So amazing and kind.

Words of gratitude like Lori's keep me very clear about my work.

with paper plates and passion anything is possible

Being asked to decide between your passion for work and your passion for children was like being asked by your doctor whether you preferred him to remove your brain or your heart. — MARY KAY BLAKELY

ONE OF THE CHALLENGES FOR ANY WOMAN running a business is balancing work and home. This can be especially hard for moms. Being a mother is a gift and a powerful calling. For some moms the calling is to stay home full-time, for others it is to be a loving parent while working outside the home. For me, creating meaningful work for myself was precisely what enabled me to do the meaningful work of raising my children without going crazy.

> No one can tell you what the right choice is. You have to trust your gut and find what works for you.

stepping stone

Each choice brings out the critics. When I stayed home full-time, many women criticized me for spending my days in such a subservient way; when I worked full-time, many women criticized me for putting my career ahead of my children. Neither was the case, but it didn't matter; the sides were drawn: you were either "just" a stay-at-home mom or a "bad" working mom. Personally, I feel the best mom is a happy mom – whatever that means for you.

stepping stone

The best thing a mother can give her child is a happy and fulfilled mom. There are many paths to happiness and fulfillment, follow your heart and choose your own way.

It's rarely an easy choice to make. I have friends who have admitted to having more children simply to put off having to decide what to do with their own lives. I also know some women who seem to want their children to remain dependent on them forever so they will always feel needed. I recall starting to feel as though the burden of being home full-time was somehow forced upon me and that my children "owed" me for the sacrifice I was making on their behalf. That was a huge lightbulb moment for me. My kids hadn't asked me to stay home full-time, and they didn't owe me anything for the choice I had made to do so. It was that realization that led me to dig deep and find my voice and speak up about the fact that I wasn't happy being home full-time.

Not that it wasn't scary. Stepping out on the limb of following our dreams is almost always a frightening experience, no matter how much support we have. And often it requires enlightening the people around us.

When I asked my friend and Femail Creations artist

Joni about how she felt when she first began her business, she said:

> It took many years to find the strength, time and energy to create. My family still has a hard time taking what I do as a serious job. It always seems to surprise them when I am recognized for my painting. I had to reeducate them that I am important and have needs also, much like them. For the first few years I painted from 10:00 in the evening till about 4:00 A.M. That made my family mad also because I was so tired. But when I tried to paint regular hours, that didn't work either with carpooling, cleaning, cooking, and taking care of all their needs. I was always tired and guilty! So I found a small space in the house (half of the laundry room) and started my journey. I told them about my feelings and the plans I had for myself. And most of all I explained to them that the happier I am, the happier they will be.

I stayed home full-time with my first child until she went to school. Looking back, I don't think it was in my best interest, and I wonder if it was in hers. Frankly, she seemed a little bored with me, and I was struggling to domesticate myself. By the time my second child came along, I knew myself better. I knew I wasn't doing anybody any favors being home full-time if that wasn't where I wanted to be.

When my son was a toddler, I started working part-time. As my kids grew, so did my work hours. I believed, and still do, that raising my children is the single most important job I will ever do. I also believe I was a better mom when I also worked outside the home.

stepping stone

> *We are each unique, and what works for me won't work for you. Do what is right for you and don't listen to what everyone else has to say about it. Believe me, you and your children will both win.*

The ways women juggle work and children are as diverse as the women themselves. Cindy Morgan, owner of the Atlanta-based firm Quadras, Inc., explained her situation this way:

It was a difficult struggle once my children were born. I went from a plan of live-in help to believing I would sell to my partners when my maternal instinct seemed to leave me no options. What I eventually settled on was heading back to work ten days after the c-section birth of my first child. I had a studio nursery built and a nanny in tow, along with diapers, food, toys, etc. I breastfed during phone calls, spent hours wandering the studio with my daughter in a backpack, and learned to cram my old sixty-hour workweek into thirty hours, to allow me family time. Work rarely suffered, but I did (and often still do). I became an ultra-organized whirling dervish, and many times a tired shrew.

When Alex was six months old, I became pregnant (joyfully!) with number two, Charlotte. This meant building a new and bigger nursery at the studio, and twice the food, diapers, clean clothes, sheets, etc, to bring in each week. I had, between home and work, four cribs, two playpens, four highchairs, and more! I continued this life through Alex's kindergarten. They were in tow with me always. They took their first steps here, had their birthday parties with my employees, and included them in their good night prayers; they even shared their "potty" experiences with visiting clients.

I'm not sure what it really meant to the children – they say they don't remember much. So, was it guilt, or was it love? Will it make them safer and more secure adults? I don't know. I would do it again – I loved having them here.

One of the things that was really important to me after starting the catalog was continuing to eat dinner together every night as a family. For the first few years it was a real challenge and we had to get very creative. We literally moved our kitchen table down to the office. We also ate out a lot – okay more than a lot. You know you haven't cooked in a while when you yell, "Come and eat," and the kids all jump in the car. But to us it wasn't nearly as important what or where we ate as it was that we ate together.

Early on, my incredibly ahead-of-her-time mother-in-law taught me one of the most valuable lessons on this subject: use paper plates. Linda used paper plates at almost every meal except Sunday dinner – and even then sometimes she would just whip out the Chinet. At first, I thought this was a bit odd and frankly uneconomical, even a little indulgent, but after I had my own children, I realized just how smart this woman was. I can't begin to tell you how much of my sanity has been saved by paper plates. (And before I get letters about my wastefulness, please keep in mind all of the water I am saving by not running the dishwasher everyday!)

Seriously, paper plates are a mainstay at our house. I will

never forget seven-year-old Harlie coming home from having dinner at a friend's house and reporting, "It was really strange . . . Lauren's mom ironed the napkins and then we had to eat off these hard china plates. I didn't like it." I tried to explain that some people do things differently than we do and that is okay. But Harlie still couldn't figure out why in the world you would spend so much time cooking dinner, ironing napkins, and then washing dishes. She was baffled that Lauren's mom not only cooked so many different foods (think four-course meal), but that she also took the cuisine out of the pots and pans and served them in entirely different bowls. After years of seeing the spaghetti go straight from the stovetop to the table at our house, this was simply beyond her comprehension.

Of course, hearing this, I immediately started thinking that I was a terrible mom. It was what Harlie said next that put things back into perspective for me. She said "All Lauren's mom did was work in the kitchen, and when we asked her to play Uno with us she couldn't because she had all of those dishes to wash." As quickly as my mind went down the path of unfit mother, I realized that in my child's world, having time to play cards was far more important than what was being served and what it was being served on! It also dawned on me that for my daughter, paper plates were (and are) just "normal." In fact, we just finished eating dinner and the plates are already in the recycling bin and I am back to writing.

The point is adults should take lessons from children on adaptability. Kids are amazingly resilient and don't have nearly as many expectations as we adults do. They just want to be loved; they really, truly don't care what you make for dinner or if the house is spotless or the laundry is all done.

Getting Inspiration from Our Kids

Harlie has always been very outspoken (the apple doesn't fall far from the tree!). Parenting a kid like her can be a real challenge, but, as any parent of a precocious and strong-willed child will tell herself (over and over again!), these very attributes that can drive us so crazy are the same ones that will make our children amazing adults. Harlie has always been a trailblazer, and her courage has been a constant source of inspiration for me.

When she was younger and wanted to play hockey and there weren't any girl's teams, she played on the boy's team as the only girl in the league. She took a lot of flack for that, much of it, ironically enough, coming from the *dads* of the boys on the team, not the boys themselves. I will never forget one of the father's showing up to watch his son play for the first time. Harlie took off her helmet as she skated off the rink and all of her long blond hair tumbled out. The dad blurted out, "Hey, that's a girl?!" so loudly that everyone there heard him, including Harlie. I went over to the dad and informed him that *that girl* was my daughter, and asked him if he had a problem with her playing. Amazingly, he said yes and informed me that he would rather she put on a skirt and cheer for the boys than play with them on the team.

The game ended in a tie and went to a shoot out. Both teams put their best scorer on the line. You guessed it. The best scorer on our hockey team, much to this dad's dismay, was Harlie. She scored the winning goal. I couldn't resist walking over to the dad and asking him if he would still rather have Harlie on the sidelines in a skirt. My spirited child had once again blazed another trail. The next season she wasn't the only girl in the league.

It was actually watching my daughter grow up that really forced me to look at myself and the example I was setting for her. Harlie had certainly *heard* me say often enough that she could be anything she wanted to be and do anything she wanted to do. I always encouraged her to dream big dreams and supported her whenever she tried something new. But what message was I sending her by putting my own dreams on the back burner? Kids tend to pay more attention to what we do than what we say. How could I expect her to feel permission to follow her dreams someday when she saw me putting my own dreams on hold? That was one of the main catalysts for me to start my own business.

When I asked artist and business owner Gina Cerda what advice she would give other women who want to follow their dreams, she said, "KNOW that you can be successful. FEEL the joy in your cells. Your dreams are YOUR personal gift. Teach your children by DOING it." It was her last statement that really struck me. I think women so often look at our time working as a burden on our children when perhaps it is that very work that is a gift for our children, especially our daughters. Girls need to see, not just hear, that following our passions is important. Indeed, my daughter did watch her mother closely, and at the ripe old age of thirteen, she started her own company, Girls Rock, to encourage other girls to believe in themselves. Harlie designs T-shirts, pencils, stationery, and other products to reinforce the message that girls can do anything.

Getting out of My Own Way

I confess; sometimes I wish my daughter weren't quite as brave as she is. It gives her mom all that much more to worry about. When Harlie was about fifteen years old she went to a snowboarding camp over the holiday school break with some friends. The snowboarding coaches at the camp saw real potential in her and encouraged Harlie to get serious about her riding. So she came home and asked us if she could go to the boarding school they recommended. I said we would talk about it over dinner that night.

Jeff and I asked her a lot of questions about when the school started and how long it lasted, all the while thinking she was talking about another week-long snowboarding clinic. It wasn't until dessert arrived that we discovered she meant *boarding* school – as in live-away-from-home school. We told Harlie it was out of the question. She was only fifteen and there was no way we were going to let her go to school one thousand miles away in the mountains of Colorado.

Harlie pleaded and pointed out that we lived in the desert and there was no snow, making it very difficult to train. She had her snowboarding coach call and convince us to at least visit the school. The smaller class sizes were appealing, the location was beautiful, and the school had produced several Olympic champions. The school's academic structure allowed for the students to train and compete as skiers and snowboarders all the while getting an incredible education. But still I couldn't begin to consider letting my precious daughter move out and attend school so far away.

After weeks of begging to go, Harlie finally seemed to give up and come to terms with the fact that we weren't going to say yes. She came to me one night and told me that she understood that she wasn't going to be able to go and that she was very disappointed because she felt like I was being a hypocrite. What? How was I being a hypocrite? She reasoned that after years of telling her to follow her passion and that she could do anything she put her mind to, I was holding her back because of my own fear. At fifteen, this wise daughter of mine was using my own words against me. She said she thought the only reason I wasn't letting her go was because I was afraid. Harlie didn't think it was fair that I was allowing my desire to have her home and my own fears about letting her go prevent her from following her dreams. Ouch! She knew *I* was the one who was afraid, and she was calling me on it.

I didn't sleep at all that night. I knew she was right. But I was so scared to let her go. It was time to put my money where my mouth was and let her follow her passion, even if it was going to be painful for me. It was one of the hardest things I have ever done.

The first year Harlie was away at school, I was on the phone with her dorm mom constantly and spent more time crying than I care to admit. The second year went much better. Harlie ended up with a fabulous education that she wouldn't have gotten otherwise, graduated early, and made it to Nationals two years in a row in the half-pipe competition. Once again my daughter had shown me the way, and I am grateful I got out of my own way and let her spread her wings.

We play a huge role in who our children may ultimately become. We should never underestimate the power in giving ourselves and our children permission to follow our passions. Artist Amy Peters had this to say on the subject:

> My mother was a stay-at-home mom and I credit my creative nature to the fact that she put us in every after school art program that she could find. Since I am now a mom I realize that it was as much for her own sanity as it was for our enjoyment.
>
> When I was eight I took a class in jewelry enameling. I loved it and I was good at it. A piece of mine was chosen to be in the local art show at the community center. So I was hooked. I begged for a kiln that year for Christmas. That holiday season my whole world revolved around getting that kiln. After my jewelry enameling I went on to take classes in each and every aspect of jewelry design and creation over the years and eventually studied it in college. But I still place credit on that one Christmas present that my parents picked out for me; that kiln gave me the reassurance that my art was in fact a valuable endeavor. When I opened it that Christmas morning it held infinite possibilities for me and opened up doors of creative expression that have guided me to my dreams.

What We Learn from Our Mothers

Some of us have mothers who set an example for us about how to take the steps necessary to follow our dreams, and some of us have mothers who show us just the opposite. Whether we have brave moms who inspire us by living their own lives with courage or moms who choose to shrink away from life, we can learn from them. Knowing what we don't want out of life can be as important as knowing what we do. If your own mother didn't play the role you wanted in your life, don't let that be an excuse for limiting your possibilities or even minimizing your relationship. Maybe in your case the roles will be reversed and the first generation will learn from the second.

I wish for every woman the nurturing spirit of the following poem and the support of a strong woman and the knowledge that good mothers come in many forms. I thank author Patricia Lynn Reilly for letting me share it with you.

IMAGINE A MOTHER
Imagine a mother who believes she belongs in the
    world.
A mother who celebrates her own life.
Who is glad to be alive.
Imagine a mother who celebrates the birth of her
    daughters.
A mother who believes in the goodness of her
    daughters.
Who nurtures their wisdom. Who cultivates their
    power.
Imagine a mother who celebrates the birth of her sons.
A mother who believes in the goodness of her sons.
Who nurtures their kindness. Who honors their tears.
Imagine a mother who turns toward herself with
    interest.
A mother who acknowledges her own feelings and
    thoughts.
Whose capacity to be available to her family deepens
    as she is available to herself.

Imagine a mother who is aware of her own needs and
desires.

A mother who meets them with tenderness and grace.

Who enlists the support of respectful friends and
chosen family.

Imagine a mother who lives in harmony with her heart.

A mother who trusts her impulses to expand and
contract.

Who knows that everything changes in the fullness of
time.

Imagine a mother who embodies her spirituality.

A mother who honors her body as the sacred temple of
the spirit of life.

Who breathes deeply as a prayer of gratitude for
life itself.

Imagine a mother who values the women in her life.

A mother who finds comfort in the company of
women.

Who sets aside time to replenish her woman-spirit.

Imagine yourself as this mother.

owning our power

8

You gain strength, courage, and confidence by every experience in which you really stop to look fear in the face. You must do the thing which you think you cannot do.

— ELEANOR ROOSEVELT

I CONSTANTLY HEAR WOMEN SAY THEY CAN'T DO such and such because they don't know how. Most women would be amazed at how much they *do* know. Oftentimes the very skills required to run a home and raise children are the same skills we need to run a business and manage employees. They are the very skills we need to follow our passion. Just because we don't get paid to do housework and childrearing and aren't recognized for these contributions does not mean that they are not of value. In fact, most of the skills I brought to my business came from outside a business environment. I gained much more from years of managing a household than I did from the years I managed a construction business.

As women we set such limits on ourselves; we underestimate ourselves constantly. We're so brainwashed into thinking we need advanced degrees and specialized training to get out into the world and succeed! Take it from me. It ain't so! If I had limited myself to only the things I thought I had professional or paid experience in, I would have had a darn short list!

We women are amazing creatures! But we have to decide that we matter, that it's time to take our turn. And then we have to open ourselves up to the possibilities and own our power.

Education and business experiences aren't the only factors; in fact, they aren't even the most important factors in determining the success of any business. Hard work and determination are the most important factors. I agree with Mary Catherine Bateson, who said, "We are not what we know but what we are willing to learn." Of course, it helps to have a lot of passion, too! Passion will take you a long way. I was once being interviewed for a magazine article and the journalist asked me about how great it must be to be able to set my own hours. I laughed and told her the flexibility was great – I could pick any eighteen hours a day I wanted to work. I always tell people that when you start a business, you'd better love what you are doing and be passionate about it, because the reality is that you will spend most of your waking hours doing it – and often without much pay.

An Advanced Degree in Life Experience

Things from our past that at the time didn't seem important or related can all lead us to our ultimate goal. For many years, I volunteered at my daughter's school. My husband and I both spent one morning a week in her kindergarten class reading to the students. As she entered each new grade, my responsibilities seemed to grow as fast as she did. That is the thing about volunteering . . . once they have your name and number, they never forget it! I was everything from the room mom to head of the yearbook committee and fought hard for issues I felt really mattered for our children's education.

At times, this volunteer work was all consuming. I often worked fifty and sixty hours a week without pay. Those years helped prepare me for the future when I would again work many long hours for free trying to build my own business.

I once had a job that required me to get up in front of an audience – something I had never done before – and sell a product. Although I wholeheartedly believed in this product, I didn't consider myself a sales person and hated every minute of it. Years later that experience of having to speak in front of a group came in handy when I became the vice president of the school's Parent-Teacher Organization (remember the purple school caper?) and had to speak in front of school boards and hundreds of parents on a regular basis. In fact, it was as the vice president of the parent organization that I spoke at my first press conference and years later that I started Femail Creations and frequently found myself in front of the camera. My experiences in sales and as a volunteer community leader both helped prepare me to handle the media with some degree of confidence. You just never know which life experiences you will draw on as you follow your dream.

The truth is, it really doesn't matter what degrees you have. You can learn what you need to know for almost any business without fancy MBAs and PhDs. The only advanced degree I had when I started Femail Creations was a PhD in catalog *shopping!* The only real market research I had done was as a consumer. As a busy working mom, I did most of my shopping through catalogs, hardly the "right" business background if you follow the experts. Actually, my perspective as a catalog shopper was invaluable. When I started my business, I reflected on all the experiences – both good and bad – that I had encountered as a catalog shopper over the years and tried to eliminate as many of the negative and enhance as many of the positive elements as I could for my customers.

As I was about to take another huge step outside my comfort zone and start to write this book, I decided to ask my friend and fellow author SARK what mistakes I should avoid making. Her response: make more mistakes! True to SARK's succulence, she reminded me that experience is our best teacher. And that experience doesn't always have to come from a college degree or paying job. When asked about college, I like to borrow SARK's phrase and tell people that I went to "collage" instead. My life is a collage of experiences, and I draw wisdom from that.

Changing the Status Quo

When I decided to take a deep breath and take my turn, I was met with a variety of responses. I had people applaud my courage, I had people tell me I was nuts, I had many people tell me I was selfish. I had people in my life who were supportive, and I had people in my life who were not. Interestingly enough, it seems to press a few buttons! One of the most remarkable phenomena I encountered along the way was an overwhelming concern for my husband and how my starting a business would impact him.

I have been asked a thousand times, "What did your

husband think when you started your business?" Do our husbands get asked such questions when they launch their careers? Of course not! In fact, people often ask Jeff why he was so supportive of my "crazy idea." What he usually tells them is that he didn't think it was so crazy. He also points out that I rarely get kudos for the support I gave him when he started *his* own business ten years earlier.

No. When a woman supports her partner as he starts a company, everyone thinks it's business as usual, but when a man supports his partner as she starts a company, everyone expects cartwheels. Plain and simple, Jeff tells folks, "She was my biggest supporter when I began my business, and now it's her turn."

There is still such a double standard. But you know what? We are the only ones who can change that status quo.

I was recently doing a radio interview when the question, "How does your husband feel about you starting your own business?" came up once again. We were live on the air, but I couldn't resist replying, "My husband is very supportive of me, as I am of him. How does your wife feel about you being on the radio?" His response? "I don't know. I have never asked her."

My hope is that simply by asking the question I helped some listeners think about things in a new light. If there's one thing I've discovered, it's that it's the small things that can lead to the big shifts in thinking.

Spending Matters

One of those small things we can all do is think about where and how we spend our dollars. Ford Motor Marketing reports that women have 95 percent veto power regarding automotive purchases and *influence 80 percent of all purchases.* Think of the power in that. Remember a few chapters ago I was talking about buying more directly from artisans and not going with lower-priced items that are mass-produced oversees by people working under horrid conditions? That's the whole point. We have a tremendous amount of power in how we spend our money. We can choose to be informed about a company's human rights practices, discrimination practices, and social responsibility and decide whether or not that is where we want to spend our hard-earned money. We can choose to spend our money with women-owned businesses. Every time we spend a dollar, it is a vote for or against something.

Years ago, a huge retail chain store pulled a T-shirt from all of their stores because they felt it didn't represent their version of "family values." The T-shirt said, "Someday a Woman Will Be President." Well, their refusal to sell such a woman-empowering T-shirt didn't reflect *my* version of family values, so I stopped shopping there. Doing a bit of research, I discovered that that store's major competitor gives millions of dollars each year to breast cancer research, so that's where I choose to spend (vote with) my shopping dollars.

I remember reading about First Lady Barbara Bush's 1990 commencement address to Wellesley College, during which she said:

> And who knows? Somewhere out there in this audience may even be someone who will one day follow in my footsteps, and preside over the White House as the President's spouse. I wish him well.

We have the chance to exercise this power pretty much every day, from the smallest purchases to the largest. I recently went to my favorite little bookstore in search of a gift for my brother's birthday. I like the store because the owners really care about their customers and give back to the community. When I got there, I was surprised and so disheartened to find that they were having a going-out-of-business sale. I told the owners how much I had loved shopping at their store and asked them why they were going out of business. They said they were no longer able to compete with the major chain bookstores. They were saddened all the more, they said, about having to close their store after hearing so many of their customers say that they would have shopped there more often if they'd only known.

No one's gonna do it for us, folks. Simply by shopping at our local bookstore instead of at the mall, the people of my community could have made the difference. If we really care about where our shopping dollars go, we have to put our money where our mouth is and support those companies who share our philosophy of life. Before it is too late!

According to the U.S. Census Bureau, women make up more than half of the U.S. population. When we start to own our power in one area of our life, that sense of empowerment tends to spill over into other areas. Simple acts of courage lead to great acts of courage.

stepping stone

making a
difference

9

*Never doubt that a small group of dedicated
people can make a difference.
Indeed it is the only thing that ever has.*

— MARGARET MEAD

THE YEAR BEFORE I BEGAN FEMAIL CREATIONS my sister-in-law and friend Julie called me to tell me about a woman in Boston named Babbie Cameron who collected yarn and knitting needles to send to the women of Bosnia and Croatia so they could knit scarves and mittens and socks to stay warm. According to the article Julie had read, Babbie's project was already gathering momentum and people from all over the country were sending in yarn and knitting needles. Julie knew I would want to join in and help these women, so she clipped out the article and sent it to me with the address.

I went out that day and gathered up boxes of yarn and shipped them off.

After Femail Creations got off the ground, I thought about Babbie and wanted to somehow use the catalog to help. I contacted her and asked how we could support the great work she was doing. She said that the women now had all of the mittens, sweaters, and socks they needed, thanks to people's incredible generosity; however, she was continuing to send them supplies so that they could sell their excess clothing back to her for sale here in the United States. Babbie's generous idea, now called the Rainbow Socks Project, not only provided clothing and warmth to the women but also an income stream to help them rebuild their village, which was destroyed in the war.

I asked Babbie if we could feature the Rainbow Socks as our holiday charity in the catalog. I knew our customers would love the story and want to buy the socks and mittens and reach out to these women thousands of miles away. Babbie loved the idea and we immediately began working out the logistics of how to get that many socks over here.

Each pair of mittens or socks was knitted by hand using the patterns these women had been handing down for generations, and each woman would stitch a little piece of paper with her name on it in the mitten or sock. No two were exactly alike, but each one was a heartfelt work of art.

Women loved the whole idea of buying these socks, and we had such a great success the first year we decided to feature them again in our next holiday issue of the catalog. That year we sold even more mittens and socks. Babbie used her personal frequent flier miles to fly over to Bosnia to pick up the socks herself to guarantee that we would get them here in time to sell them for the catalog. And then she did the same thing again when she brought the women their check from Femail Creations.

The women in Bosnia were able to reconstruct their

village with the money we sent them from the mittens and socks we sold in the catalog.

When Babbie returned from Bosnia, she sent me a gift I truly treasure, a letter and a piece of cloth. The letter explained that the piece of cloth was the first one produced by the loom they bought for the village, using the money Femail Creations sent them. Babbie said they all called me the "good woman," and told her to take this to the "good woman" who helped them rebuild their village.

From the very beginning, I wanted the catalog to give back and to reach out to other women – that was the whole point. One of the ways we do that is to feature a charity like the Rainbow Socks project in every single issue of the catalog. We not only share with our customers the story of the charity and the wonderful work it is doing, we also donate a portion of the proceeds from that catalog directly to that charity. Our Making a Difference program brings much needed awareness and funding to these charities. The more Femail Creations grows, the more we can give back. It is what keeps me excited about growing the business, even when that means increasing my workload. Meaningful work is still work, after all, and still comes with the same risks any other business does. The difference is that the work is fulfilling on so many more levels.

A few years ago, I was at a convention for the catalog industry, trying to figure out this strange business I was in. One of the sessions offered was an Executive Forum, a somewhat informal moderated discussion. About fifty executives gathered around a huge table discussing some of the challenges of the mail order industry, including rising paper and postage costs, distribution, circulation, and tricky inventory forecasting. Most of the catalogs were much larger than Femail Creations, and it really was informative to hear how they faced the formidable task of managing their companies.

As the session began to wrap up, I took my chance to ask a time management question that had been bothering me for some time. I stood up and asked the other catalog owners how they handled all of the letters and email from customers. It was clear by the looks on their faces that they weren't even quite sure what I meant! So I clarified by asking how they handled the volume and if they still answered all of their own email personally. One gentleman gave me a patronizing look and explained that, of course, customer service complaints are dealt with by the customer service department. Others around the table all nodded in agreement.

Now it was my turn for the puzzled look. I wasn't referring to complaints. I was talking about positive feedback! When I told them about all the notes my customers email me about how Femail Creations has touched their lives, they looked positively dumbfounded.

When the woman conducting the session broke the awkwardness by asking if anyone else had such a cheery challenge, there was only laughter in the room. It was at this point that I realized just what a unique position I was in to be blessed with such a "problem." I realized that this kind of business model really is different.

I may not have understood all of the executive panel's analytical discussions, but I did leave that meeting with the knowledge that to customers the heart of a company matters as much as its brains. I realized then just how much Femail Creations truly resonated in the lives of our customers. Whether we made a penny or not, our mission had indeed been a success. We were making a difference in the lives of our customers. And we are lucky enough to get to hear about it!

Reaching Out

We can each make a difference. And you just never know how one simple act on your part might affect another person. Each month, we send Free Stuff from Femail Creations to one of our customers, who fills out our Web site survey asking customers to share their insights with us. Several years ago, I got a letter from one of those survey winners thanking me for sending her the gifts. Her letter still gives me goose bumps whenever I think about it. In it, she described that her outlook on life had become incredibly bleak; in fact, she had given up and decided to end her own life. But a knock at her door changed her plans. When for some reason she decided to answer the door, it was the UPS driver handing her a box labeled Free Stuff. She opened the box and immediately came upon a ceramic tile that said, "Have faith, tides will change . . ." She realized in that instant that if a perfect stranger could reach out and send her the exact words she needed to hear, then maybe things in her life could indeed get better. She decided right then and there that she was going to live after all. My little catalog actually saved a life!

That story may seem like one in a million, but the fact is all of us can use our experiences and our resources, however limited, to reach out and help others. Victoria Rowell, one of the stars on the top-rated show *The Young and The Restless,* grew up in the foster care system as a child. She was given the opportunity to take classical ballet lessons at the age of eight, and on this wonderful beginning, she was able to base her now flourishing career as a dancer and actress. Victoria is committed to giving other foster children the opportunity that was afforded her by her foster mother, the late Agatha Armstead, the Ford Foundation, and the mentors she encountered along the way.

In 1990, Victoria Rowell started the Rowell Foster Children's Positive Plan, a scholarship fund dedicated to helping foster children thrive through fine arts, sports, and job opportunities. Victoria and Femail Creations teamed up to create a special pillow we could offer in the catalog to provide funds in support of Victoria's foundation. Victoria chose to use her life experiences to reach out and help others. I know I feel supported all the time by the generosity of spirit of my customers. They have given this catalog wings to fly, when in reality she should never have gotten off the ground.

You can do it, too!

stepping stone | **We each can – and do – make a difference!**

the juggling act 10

Women are a lot like tea bags. They never know how strong they are until they get into hot water.
— ELEANOR ROOSEVELT

WOMEN ARE SO GOOD AT SO MANY THINGS WE often end up doing way too much. Because we can, we do. I have often joked that most women I know could easily work for the circus; we are so good at juggling it all. For years I had this mental image of myself as one of those plate spinners trying to keep each area of my life going – all at the same time – without letting any of the plates come crashing to the ground. I am here to tell you that is not a good way to live. If you are trying to spin too many plates, sooner or later one of them is bound to hit you right smack in the head.

It wasn't long after I started my own business that I realized that I was getting smacked in the head by all those plates. I was no longer a "well-rounded person." One by one, things started falling away. Gone were lunch dates with the girls, gone were my monthly manicures, gone were the books I loved to read for pure pleasure, gone were our couples' nights out with friends, and long gone were vacations. I was becoming two-dimensional. The only things I had (or made) time for in my life were my family and work. It remained that way for many years.

Bringing Work Home

In an effort to get out of the office to spend time with my family, I used to bring home work almost every night, figuring I could do it after they went to bed. I rationalized that they wouldn't miss me while they were asleep! The flaw in that logic, of course, was that I didn't leave any time for my own sleep. Like a good girl, I was always willing to sacrifice to make time for everyone else. Bad idea! Sleeping isn't for wimps; it's for folks who like to stay sane!

Initially I brought my work home in one of the totes we carried in the catalog, but one day the spreadsheets and catalog proofs and paperwork simply wouldn't fit in the tote, so I grabbed one of the plastic storage tubs we used in the warehouse. From that day on, a blue tub would come home with me each night. I thought this was a fine system, but almost immediately the office staff and my family, especially my daughter, started making fun of my tub. My daughter begged me to get a "real briefcase" or something a little less embarrassing than a plastic storage bin. I didn't give up the tub easily. Finally, for Mother's Day one year, my family got me a more professional-looking workbag and I reluctantly gave up my blue tub.

It turns out my new briefcase could hold a lot of work! One night as I was leaving the office, I put the bag on the seat next to me. As I starting backing out of the parking space, I noticed a red light on my dashboard that I had never seen before. It was the passenger seat belt light! Apparently, my briefcase weighed so much that the car registered it as a passenger and was alerting me that she needed to buckle up. Now, when your briefcase is so heavy it sets off the seat belt light, you know you are bringing home way too much work! Talk about a light-bulb moment! I knew it was time to find a way to get more balance into my life.

Finding a Little Balance

At that point, I was still designing and producing the catalog. That job tended to be my night shift, and I was wearing out. I was never really that technical to begin with and had only learned how to produce the catalog out of financial necessity. But I knew I couldn't keep doing it forever. It was time, beyond time, to find a real graphic artist. One of the other staff members recommended that I try a local woman she knew. It turned out to be a great fit and she did a wonderful job for us for many years.

It was also a great lesson in letting go. When I first contemplated hiring a graphic artist after three years of doing the catalog myself, I just didn't think I'd be able to hand that baby over to somebody else. I was so close to the project, and I worried that no one else would ever "get" my creative vision. Much to my surprise, it was easy, and that gave me some badly needed reassurance that I really *could* delegate and let go.

When the fabulous organization Mothers in Business contacted me and asked me to speak at one of their monthly gatherings, I was honored by the request, until I found out what the topic was. They wanted me to speak on finding balance! Me! My first thought was, "Oh no, I am the wrong person for that. I am certainly no expert on balance!" But I grabbed my calendar anyway to see if we could come up with a date. As I looked over my schedule, the irony of the whole thing just stared me in the face. I hadn't had a single day off in over a month. But I agreed to a date and was determined to have *something* useful to say by then. I shared my predicament with my friend Lexy, who also owned her own business, and she said, "Just tell them the truth. They'll find it refreshing to know they are not alone. I know I would!"

Over the next week, I kept thinking about what I could share with this group, what I could possibly say that would inspire them or help them find balance.

The morning of the speaking engagement, my sister Cynthia called while I was driving to the office. When I told her I was on my way to give a speech on balance, she laughed out loud! She said, "Why would they ask you to speak on *that?*" She then said something really valuable. She said she has found that balancing life is like standing on a balance beam. You must keep moving your arms and adjusting your body to find the center and then readjust to find it again and again.

That's really true. I used to associate tranquility and stillness with balance, but balance is more about fluid motion. There's a lot of movement and adjusting involved. In fact, if you hold perfectly still you are more likely to fall off the beam. On top of that, what works today won't tomorrow, and each situation and person will require a bit of adjusting to find the center again. Hour by hour, day by day, balance is about finding our center again and again and again.

What I discovered is that my old idea of balance is,

well, out of balance. Think about it. There's no such thing as perfect balance. If you picture your life as a big cheesecake (I like that better than pie!), with a slice for everything that you feel is important – a slice for your family, for your friends, for your work, for play, for spirituality, for rest, for all of the things that matter to you – you can see how futile it is to try to make all the slices the same size all the time. Life just doesn't work that way, and that's okay. Sometimes your family will have a bigger slice, sometimes work will have a bigger slice, sometimes sleep is just a sliver! The important thing is to remember to get a taste of each slice of the cake. They may not be equal in size, but they're all important.

All Work and No Play

One of the ways I carve out time for the relaxation piece of my cheesecake is by running away from time to time. I simply can't do the balance thing day by day – you know, leaving work at a "reasonable" hour, not bringing it home, and all. I have to pretty much burn out and then run away for a few days to recover. After years of trying to balance work and play, it's the only thing that works for me. Actually, it took my husband kidnapping me for a weekend to learn that lesson. After deadline upon deadline, exhaustion had set in, and my husband could see there was no end in sight. So he took matters into his own hands and whisked me away to the beach for the weekend.

It was the best gift he could have given me. And it was a lesson that stays with me to this day. Someday I may be able to hang out at home without the internal nag calling me back to work, but for now, I consider myself on probation.

For now, I have to get out of town from time to time just to stay sane. Sleep and time off really do make us all much more pleasant to be around.

A Woman's Work Is Never Done

The truth is there will always be more to do. No one can juggle it all, but we can juggle some. The key to a successful juggling act is getting some of the tasks off the to-do list. And to do that we have to let go of our need for perfection and allow others to carry their weight.

Those of us in relationships with male partners, in particular, often end up carrying much more of the burden than our mates do. There is a reason we need a purse and they can get by with a wallet! Men tend to have tunnel vision. When they are at work, they think about work.

For women it doesn't quite work like that. When we are at work, we are thinking about work . . . and our kids, what to get our nephew for his birthday, how our daughter is doing at college, the fact we need to schedule a pap smear before our birth control pills run out, our guilt about not writing our grandma a letter this week, our friend who is going through a divorce, our son's homework project that is due tomorrow, what we are going to make for dinner that night . . . and work.

And, by the way, don't fool yourself. Women play a big role in the imbalance. I often hear women say they would rather do all the __ (fill in the blank: laundry, grocery shopping, gift buying) because they want it done *their way*. I have a friend who won't let her husband do the laundry because she doesn't like how he folds the towels! Personally, I don't care if my towels are folded like origami as long as they are clean and I wasn't the one who had to wash, dry, and put them away.

We must let go of the notion that we are the only ones capable of doing domestic things the "right" way. Isn't the right way the way that gets it done? We are doing our partners and our children a huge disservice if we don't allow them to do their share. No, I don't love how my son unloads the dishwasher. Yes, I would rather not find the blender with the pots and pans and the salad spinner in the towel drawer. However, Bridger is catching on that it doesn't matter how poorly he puts the dishes away; the job is still going to be his to do, and as a consequence, he is actually getting better at it. I'm even confident that over time we won't need a GPS to find our cereal bowls!

Women still tend to think of men as "helping" around the house and "baby-sitting" their children. The very fact that we call it "help" indicates that we still feel that the primary burden of caring for the home and children is ours. Imagine if you called a friend to go to dinner and she said she couldn't because she had to "baby-sit" her own children that night, or couldn't go because she had to "help" around the house. Wouldn't that sound a little odd?

We have all heard women discussing tactics to get their husbands to help around the house. Frustration over this issue is nothing new. My own mother wrote an Op-Ed piece to a local newspaper when I was a child, addressing the same issue. That was a long time ago, but not nearly enough has changed.

I cringe when I hear a woman say she "just stays home." As if there was anything simple or easy about that! I personally think staying home full-time is the hardest job on the planet and one that never gets the respect it deserves.

I look at it this way; one partner went to work outside the home all day and one partner went to work inside the home all day. However, all too often when the partner who worked outside of the home returns there is a sense that their day is done. But when does the day end for the partner who worked at home all day? Because they never leave the "office," their job seems to go on twenty-four hours a day. Wouldn't it be fairer if at the end of the workday both partners split the domestic evening shift?

If you're waiting for men to be the driving force for change, however, you are probably going to be waiting a long time. And honestly, who can blame them? They have had it pretty good, and the motivation to alter things just may not be there. Nope. We have to change *our own way* of thinking. We have to change the way we feel about the division of labor in the home and not only insist that all home chores be more evenly shared but also be willing to share them! And often that will mean letting men do things differently without complaint.

It's important to remember, of course, that having an egalitarian relationship doesn't necessarily mean a fifty-fifty split. Sometimes, whether because of extra work responsibilities, illness, or whatever, one partner will do more than the other of one task or another. Sometimes I do 80 percent of the household work and childcare and Jeff does 20 percent, but sometimes he's the one doing 80 percent and I am the one doing 20 percent. That flexibility is key to an egalitarian relationship.

Years ago, when my husband started his business, I had more time and I did most of the domestic work. When I started my business, that balance shifted, and my husband started doing most of the domestic work. Rarely has it been evenly divided on any given day, but over time it has *felt* equal, and that's what's important.

One of the ways we make it work is that we have what we call "calendar meetings" at least once a week to keep track of who is juggling what. Jeff brings his Palm Pilot and I bring my calendar and we sit down together to discuss who is picking up our son Bridger from football, who is getting the birthday present for an upcoming party he has been invited to, or which one of us is going to ship the care package off to our daughter in college. Mapping out who will be driving carpool, picking up the dry cleaning, or taking the kids to get their teeth cleaned goes a long way toward clarifying the division of labor and avoiding last-minute scrambling and frustration. We also use our calendar meeting to schedule time away for ourselves, whether that is a weekend away or a dinner date.

Creating more equilibrium in our homes brings about its own reward. Personally, I think one of the greatest benefits is the impact this has on our children. My son will never be confused about whether or not men should be doing the laundry or dishes. He has watched his Dad do that his entire life, so for him that's the norm, and I can only hope that he will take that attitude with him out into the world and into his own relationships. The same is true for our daughter, who certainly has higher expectations of men and relationships than many of her friends. In changing the way we think about our own roles, we can shift the paradigm. We often get what we expect, and we can choose to expect more.

True balance for me means making sure I create time to enjoy each slice of my cheesecake, just not necessarily all at the same time. When one piece has been the biggest piece for a long time, I start to feel out of balance and I know it's time to give another piece a turn.

Even too much adventure can throw you out of balance. I travel all around the country to find the creative merchandise in the catalog, to visit our fulfillment center, to speak at conferences, and to attend conventions. People always tell me how much they envy my jet-set life. But after too many consecutive trips, I begin to lose my equilibrium. I know I have been on the road too much when I dial nine to get an outside line on my home phone! Time to put the suitcase away for a while.

Traveling with the Drill Sergeant

Unfortunately, my work requires me to juggle a heavy travel schedule, so I am always looking for ways to make the trips more tolerable. For me the secret is a sense of humor – and a sister. Cynthia often travels with me as my shopper extraordinaire. She is the perfect complement to me. Her taste is similar enough to mine to give the catalog a certain coherence but just different enough to offer up a fresh perspective. We have a lot of fun together, and having her along makes the burden of being on the road so much easier to take.

Over the years, I have learned how to travel without abusing myself or those who travel with me. Notice I said I have *learned* this. As my sister will be the first to tell you, it was not always that way! When I first began traveling for work, I would spend all day at the show and then come back to my hotel and start my second shift. After all, being on the road didn't make my day job go away. I'd spend long nights on my laptop answering email and finishing paperwork until the wee hours of the morn. Then the alarm would go off at 6:00 A.M. to start the whole crazy cycle again.

Once, after several long days on the road, we were both so exhausted that we got in an elevator and waited several *minutes* to arrive at our floor before realizing that we'd never pushed the button. Cynthia finally threatened a mutiny if I didn't stop torturing her with my twenty-hour days. She understood my workload and hence my schedule, but she didn't want to keep it too.

I finally got a clue and learned how to travel more humanely. I no longer force us out of bed at the crack of dawn to get to the show the minute it opens. And we no longer stay at the shows until they turn the lights out. Now we get up when we get up and we leave when our feet can't take anymore.

Interestingly enough, we still find just as many wonderful artists and creative merchandise as we did back in the days of gift show boot camp. Part of me knows it's because we are getting better at it, and part of me knows it is because we are being rewarded for evolving and treating ourselves better.

"Badge-Worthy" Adventures

Over the years, Cynthia and I have had many adventures touring around the country. We eventually had so many funny encounters that we started our own little tradition to keep track of them all. We usually have to wear a badge when we attend a gift show, so I started making notes on our badges to remind us of the highlights of each trip and collecting all of the badges so we could look back and have a laugh. Now during a trade show, we will find ourselves saying that something is "badge worthy," meaning it's worth recording on our badges for posterity.

During a gift show in Philadelphia, the fire alarm at our hotel went off in the middle of the night – three nights in a row! – fortunately, each one a false alarm. On one of our trips to Atlanta, we got a big surprise when we checked in to the hotel there. The front desk staff gave us the key to our room, and upon entering, we discovered we weren't the only ones they had checked into that same room. There were other people in there! Once while in New York, we spotted a man playing a guitar in Times Square – wearing nothing but his white brief underwear and cowboy boots! You can bet that ended up on the badge!

Our travels in search of new artists and unique merchandise are never dull. We had another badge-worthy event just a few months after 9-11. We found ourselves having to travel to the craft market. Understandably, everyone was still a little jumpy and traveling was nothing anyone was taking lightly. After a long day at the show, we crawled into bed exhausted. I was awakened at first light by what sounded like a helicopter outside our window. The noise was so loud it rattled our windows and scared the wits out of me. I jumped out of bed and pulled back the curtains to see what in the world was going on. There at eye level was an enormous helicopter hovering in front of my window. I didn't know what it was doing there, but I could plainly see that the pilot had dark hair and a mustache. That's how close this chopper was to my window!

I tried to rouse Cynthia out of bed to come look, but once I had established that we weren't under siege she seemed much more interested in catching a few extra minutes of shuteye. I didn't think anyone would believe what I was seeing, so I ran to my bag and grabbed a camera. We happened to have a big window over our bathtub, so I climbed inside the tub and took a quick snapshot of this bizarre-looking orange chopper.

As I stared out the window in disbelief, a huge metal box, about the size of a semi truck, swung by the window. This scene was getting weirder by the minute. I later learned that they were refurbishing an old building across the street and the helicopters were lifting the massive air conditioning units to the rooftop. Definitely badge worthy!

We were stuck in Philly when the Blizzard of 2003 hit. We thought we were going to barely miss it and had packed up to head for the airport when the hotel called to tell us we best stay put, as there were no flights landing or departing. We watched the news as local people gathered up supplies like the world was coming to an end and this was their last chance to shop. Growing up in Utah, we couldn't imagine how a little snow could cause so many problems. Of course, that was *before* the storm hit. Once the white stuff started to fall, it didn't stop for three long days. All of the stores and restaurants were closed, and we were stuck in our room without even a mini bar. We rummaged through our suitcases and came up with a bag of peanuts, a few pieces of chocolate, and a few sticks of gum. We holed up in our peach hotel room just waiting for the airport to reopen, all the while wishing we had followed the lead of the locals when they (the smart ones!) did stock up on provisions.

As claustrophobic as that peach room started to feel, we were grateful we weren't trapped at the airport as many were. At least we had a bed and a shower and a TV to watch the news and an entire season worth of MTV's *Battle of the Sexes*. My teenage daughter couldn't believe I was actually watching that, but desperate times call for desperate measures! When the restaurants finally opened again (thanks to the employees willing to brave the snow-packed roads), we ate like we hadn't seen food in three days – well, then again, we hadn't!

Ironically, since we returned from our Blizzard of 2003 trip, there have been many times when juggling it all has felt like just too much, and we have jokingly longed to be cooped up in our peach room with nowhere to go.

Our travels have been full of other kinds of surprises as well. Never having been a big-city girl, I was surprised when I fell in love with New York. I end up there at least once or twice a year on business. That city is so full of rich diversity and culture. Our trips there are always adventure filled – none more so than the trip we just returned from. We had just finished having a late lunch when the power went out. At first we thought it was just in the restaurant we were eating at, but as we stepped outside, it was clear the entire block was without power. As we walked the four or five blocks back to our hotel in Times Square, we realized it was far worse than that. The streets were filled with frantic crowds. People poured from the subway with looks of horror on their faces. We soon learned the power was out across the East Coast.

We were stuck, like so many others, without power in the hot and humid summer weather of New York, desperately trying to find a way home. When we talked to folks on the West Coast, they would report to us that the news was saying the airports were open and flights were departing. Once we got through to the airlines, we found out that wasn't the case at all. Ultimately, with the help of our sister Diane in Phoenix (where the power was on and the phones worked) we got a car service from Connecticut to come and pick us up and drive us back there. We spent the night in Connecticut, where we finally got our first meal in a few days. Then we flew out from there, and after two long days, made it home. That was definitely badge worthy!

It seems to be a running joke with my sister and me whenever we travel together. Without fail, when we check in to whichever hotel we are staying at, our room is not ready or they don't have one or they have lost our reservation. One or both of us usually ends up with a flight delay or cancellation. Neither of us seems to have these troubles when we travel with anyone else, but get us together and it turns into a string of missed flights and mediocre hotel rooms. This year alone we have managed to get stuck in the storm of 2003 *and* the power outage of 2003. It's a good thing we can laugh about it!

We have had some amazing road trips on our quest to find unique merchandise. We have met many wonderful artists and had many laughs, many tears, and more scary cab rides than I care to count. Instead of coming back to our hotel room and just complaining about our tired feet, we have learned that after a long day at a gift show, we come back to our hotel room, complain about our tired feet – and then order room service and a movie and end a bad day on a happy note.

Cynthia also likes to drag me off to see historical sites while we are on the road – sore feet or not, she wants to get in her hour or two as a tourist in each city we visit.

She insisted we see the Liberty Bell, if for no other reason than our father is a history teacher and she felt it was our duty. For reasons I still can't explain, I let her talk me into walking miles (in freezing temperatures, I might add!) to see Elfin Alley, the oldest in the country. Sometimes her sightseeing spirit is a great thing; other times it is the last thing you want to do after spending all day at a show on your feet. I confess most of the time I end up thanking her for the change of pace and the change of scenery.

More Juggling Tricks

With so much to manage at times, all of our to-do lists can feel overwhelming. I'm happy to share another discovery about juggling it all: the good uses of procrastination. Now, I know it may feel foreign to think of procrastination as a good thing, but I have learned you can actually use this as a tool to get things done. In fact, you might be amazed at what you can accomplish while trying to avoid doing something else. I'm not promoting procrastination, of course, just saying that we can make the best of it when we're in the midst of it.

I have been known to clean out a closet to delay having to make those final merchandise decisions. I would rather wash sheets than study spreadsheets! Next time you are really dreading a project, simply do something else you have been putting off. Sooner or later, I know I will have to get to those spreadsheets, but in the hours or days I manage to put it off, I will enjoy my tidy drawers and fresh linens.

Freeing Up Brain Space

Feel a little overwhelmed at the idea of catching up with your life? You know that look little kids get when they are sent to clean their room – that utter sense of overwhelm? They don't know what to do first – pick up the toys on the floor, the piles of stuff under the bed, the clothes spilling out of the drawers. Where oh where to begin? That's what the prospect of catching up feels like to me. I feel positively engulfed by all that has to get done. I find my way out of that feeling by tackling things in bite-sized chunks. If I looked at the really big picture all of the time, I wouldn't get out of bed in the morning. Sometimes it is best to look at things in micro-movements.

From my mother I inherited the need to make lists. Some see this as a gift, others as a curse. I find that keeping lists help free up space in my brain. I know folks who can't manage without their Palm Pilots, but for me a good old calendar and a few sticky notes go a long way. I keep a Post-it in the front of my calendar, where I list the things that must get done that day. At a glance, I can see what my priorities are for that day, and as I accomplish each one, I cross it off the list. If I don't get it all done, I have learned not to beat myself up; I just put it on tomorrow's yellow Post-it. These little Post-its are vital for me to manage the various slices of my cheesecake. I find juggling life and eating cheesecake best when taken one slice at a time.

trusting our guts

11

*Every time you don't follow your inner
guidance, you feel a loss of energy, loss of power,
a sense of spiritual deadness.*

— SHAKTI GAWAIN

IN ONE OF THE EARLY YEARS OF THE CATALOG, I WAS
contacted by a woman who said she wanted to invest in
Femail Creations. It turned out she was a very well-known
businesswoman who had recently sold the business she
started from scratch for hundreds of millions of dollars.
She said she was looking for a company to invest in that
shared her passion to support other women. She asked to
meet with me so she could learn more about my catalog
business and how she might help as an angel investor.

I created a business outline to review with her in great
hopes that she might well be the investor we had been
waiting for. As my husband recalls all too well, I was a nervous wreck the day I was scheduled to meet with Pamela.
She arrived in a long, black stretch limousine and strolled
into the office. She was a tall, regal blonde woman with a
larger-than-life presence. She said she wanted to hear
every detail of my story and how I came to start a mail-
order business. Pamela seemed a little phony to me, but

I wanted to believe she was genuinely interested in supporting the mission of Femail Creations. My gut told me something was fishy, but I was desperate for an infusion of cash at the time, and her visit gave me hope that there was an investor out there who wanted to make a difference as much as she wanted to make money.

After our meeting, Pamela requested more information and then said she would be back in touch. I waited and waited to hear back from her, but my calls were not returned. In fact it would be months before I would see Pamela again – at a cataloging convention in Florida. Turns out Pamela wasn't interested in financing Femail Creations at all; she was just trying to gain the knowledge I had learned the hard way. She was at the convention because she had recently started her own catalog.

What was so heartbreaking was that a woman with her vast financial resources, who could so easily afford to hire experts, was trying to take advantage of a struggling company. What could have been such a great opportunity for us to collaborate turned into a bad experience instead. Just imagine what we could have accomplished with her experience and funding and my passion for Femail Creations and loyal customer base!

Here I had been so afraid to meet this woman, and in the end it was she who needed me! So, what did I learn? To trust my guts and honor my intuition. At that first meeting, my gut had told me that something didn't feel authentic, that she seemed like a phony. But I had put more trust in her reputation than in my own instincts. Intuition is a great resource, but it doesn't do us any good if we don't listen to it.

Honoring Our Instincts

A firm believer in karma, I was not surprised when a year later I was told that Pamela's catalog wasn't doing so well. In the end, her daughter and business partner called me to ask if I wanted to buy any of their overstock since they were going out of business. As politely as I could, I let her know that I wasn't interested. I explained that our merchandise selections were not compatible with theirs, as our focus was on supporting artisans who handcraft their work rather than importing for the lowest price and highest profit.

We can all think of times when we should have trusted intuitive information. Whether the answer or outcome is always what we want it to be or not, being true to ourselves is always the right choice, if only because it honors our own knowing.

Believe me, I've learned the hard way just how painful the consequences can be when you don't. Many years ago, I had an employee I felt I couldn't trust. She didn't report to me directly, but I had spent enough time with her to know that something just didn't seem right.

I went to her supervisor and asked how she felt things were going. She said she thought everything was fine. I left that meeting with an awful feeling, but I decided to trust her supervisor and not take any action. I justified ignoring my gut by telling myself that, being closer to her work, her supervisor would know best. Sadly, I would later learn just how right my intuition had been. It turned out this employee had been embezzling thousands of dollars from the company. Talk about learning the hard way!

Business owner Lori Bujai shared with me that her biggest obstacle is always self-doubt.

> Am I doing the right thing? Am I offering the right products? Will anyone understand what I am trying to say with my work? The best decisions I make and the best products I offer are the ones that feel good to me. Something deep down in my gut says it's the right thing to do, and when I listen, my instincts are usually right.

Using Intuition as a Forecasting Tool

Even inventory forecasting can be less a matter of mathematical projections than intuition. Over the years, as the catalog grew and sales increased, I decided there had to be a better way to determine how much inventory to hold. We looked into inventory-forecasting software, met with consultants, and dreamed up our own spreadsheets to help project inventory needs. I finally gave in and decided to hire an industry "expert" to help me out.

She flew out and we reviewed past sales and current product, and she promised to send me a report outlining her forecasts and taking this awesome responsibility off my plate once and for all. When she sent me her report with her recommended quantities for our purchase orders, my jaw dropped. Was she serious? I went back and reviewed my own numbers and was bewildered at the huge gap between what I thought we should order and what she was suggesting. Some of her numbers seemed way too high, others too low. How could we be this far apart?

I began to question my own intelligence and my own judgment, but it was past time to place our purchase orders and I couldn't wait any longer to decide on quantities. Ultimately, I decided to trust my gut and go with my own numbers. But I hung on to her recommendations so that after all was said and done, I could review to see who was actually closer. I figured I might learn something from her about inventory forecasting.

Once the sales numbers came in and I had the chance to go back and compare her recommendations to my orders, I was overjoyed. My numbers, it turns out, were right on the money. I hadn't learned much about inventory forecasting from my "expert," but I had learned a valuable lesson about trusting my gut.

I once heard this great quote by corporate motivator Sandy Linver:

> Successful executives and effective leaders are open to feedback; they use it to explore where they are both intellectually and emotionally, and how that relates to who they want to be and need to be in their world; but they don't let it shape who they are. They know that all of the really important answers are inside themselves.

It's easy to underestimate yourself and how much you've learned along the way when you're just starting out. I may not have been an inventory expert, but I was an expert on my own customers and their shopping habits. That is not to say I don't get it wrong sometimes – I certainly do – but I have come to know that I can *and should* follow what my gut tells me. I now honor the idea that I will come closer to knowing what my customers want than any stranger will, no matter what their title or level of expertise. Of course, I still fantasize about having that inventory forecasting crystal ball and ordering exactly what we need each time so we never have overstock and we always have exactly what our customers want when they want it. Sans crystal ball, I am choosing to go with my gut.

bold, barefoot, and building a business

12

The universe is made up of stories, not of atoms. — MURIEL RUKEYSER

M Y KIDS ARE ALWAYS TRYING TO GET ME TO GO bungee jumping. I keep trying to explain to them I have already taken a big leap, and frankly, I don't need anymore adrenaline flowing through my veins, thanks. I always tell people that if they really need some added excitement in their lives, they should start a business.

All of us battle-weary business owners have our tales to tell, and I think it's important for us to share our ups and our downs, our miseries not yet mastered, and our lessons learned. Trying to run a business is not easy, and for women in particular there are a lot of obstacles to overcome and challenging issues to face. Sharing our truths and being willing to open ourselves up and tell our stories is vital. If we can't commiserate and laugh together along the way, we will miss out on some invaluable wisdom.

When I speak around the country, women always come

up to me afterward and tell me they feel so much better knowing they are not alone. They say, "I thought I was the only one who struggled with such and such" or "I thought I was the only one who hadn't cooked in ages" or "I thought I was the only one who felt like I didn't know what I was doing." After each speech, it is my honesty that people tell me they find so refreshing.

The Unique Challenges of Being a Woman in Business

what to wear

I am often asked to do public speaking, and my daughter, Harlie, has assigned herself the job of making sure I look right when I do it. Every time I am asked to speak, the first thing Harlie asks is what I am going to wear. After all, in her mind if I don't use these invites as an excuse to get a new outfit, what's the point?

Sometimes I get lucky and she comes home on break in the nick of time, but the rest of the time she phones it in from college. I am sure the people at the stores I shop in think I'm crazy, always talking to myself in the dressing room. The truth is Harlie is usually on the other end of my cell phone picking out my speaking engagement outfits remotely.

When the American Marketing Association asked me to speak in 2002, Harlie happened to be home for spring break. It was a nice treat to actually have her present in the dressing room instead of on the other end of a cell phone. After trying on a dozen things, we finally settled on a new suit and headed home to make sure the shoes and shirt I had in my closet would match. It was a go.

Now all she had left to do was pick out my jewelry. Of

course, with a catalog full of jewelry, I always have plenty to choose from. We were all set.

The next morning, however, the universe had a surprise in store for me. When I went to put on the approved ensemble, I noticed a bulge in the jacket. Sticking out of my armpit was a huge white security sensor that the clerk at the store had forgotten to take out. I don't know why we didn't notice it sooner (or why we hadn't set off the alarm as we left the store!), but I did know that I was in a real pickle since I had to speak in about an hour and, as usual, the rest of my "presentable" wardrobe was at the dry cleaners.

Cursing myself for not picking up my dry cleaning sooner, I woke Harlie up to show her my predicament and beg her to race back to the store with the receipt and ask them to remove the sensor before I stood up in front of the AMA crowd looking like a shoplifter.

Being the good sport Harlie is, she raced to the mall and stood outside waiting for the store to open. What happened next still amazes me. When Harlie went to the counter and showed the clerk the receipt and the jacket and asked for the sensor to be removed, they told her they didn't have the device to remove it! Didn't have the device to remove it? What? Why the hell would they be selling jackets at their store with sensors in them if they didn't have the gadget to remove them?

Now, I don't want to give this sensor remover–deprived store a black eye, so I won't mention their name, unless of course that means I will get free clothes from one of their competitors! Suffice it to say, Harlie wasn't exactly pleased. She explained the urgency to the manager on duty, who then began running around the mall to other stores asking if she could please use their security device to remove the tag. Oddly enough, there is some rule against sharing these gadgets among stores, so that plan didn't work.

Next, the store manager called her other stores to see if any of them had the jacket in the right size without a security sensor sticking out. No luck. By this time, Harlie was starting to steam, and she made it clear that her mother was going to have this jacket back, minus sensor, in the next fifteen minutes or there would be hell to pay.

Desperate times must call for desperate measures because the next thing Harlie knew the manager had magically appeared from the back room holding a jacket in my size – sans sensor. Harlie called from her cell phone to let me know she was en route with the jacket.

We did a handoff in the garage and I raced off to give my speech. I arrived a little late and plenty frazzled and decided the only thing to do was to tell the truth. I have always been the type of gal who tells it like it is. So I shared the story of my wild morning with the audience. The women in the crowd laughed till they had tears rolling down their cheeks; the men didn't quite get it. I guess that to guys once you've seen one suit you've seen them all. But for women, getting dressed for public appearances can be a monumental task, requiring the endurance of a dressing room marathon and the luck of the shopping goddess to shine upon you – not to mention the pressure to have a good hair day!

what to eat

Excuse me, guys, but I need to share just one more gripe with the gals. Why didn't anyone tell me sooner that fat and sugar when combined with stress hormones creates cellulite? That little fact would have been nice to know about five years before I started living on French fries, chocolate, and red Swedish Fish. I am convinced I wouldn't have survived without red Swedish Fish for the first few years of the catalog. If you don't know about red Swedish Fish, you are missing out on the ultimate chewy candy treat. I think I truly became addicted. I thought I might need a twelve-step program for Swedish Fish addiction there for a while. To make matters worse, I became like a peddler and tracked down my own source for Swedish Fish and started selling them in the catalog just to be sure I would never run out.

Much to my surprise, I was not alone in my addiction. We offered the red fish in five-pound boxes and sold hundreds and hundreds of them. Now I have my Swedish Fish addiction under control and only enjoy them occasionally, although my family will out me and tell you that I still like to keep a stash handy at all times and never travel without them, just in case. It's like comfort food.

Speaking of food, fast food was my only actual food source for a long time. In the early years I used to get excited if I got out of the office early (early in the morning) enough to make it to the only fast food joint in our area that didn't close at midnight. If I made it out of the office before 3:00 A.M. I could still make it to Taco Bell for "dinner" on my way home. I can't count how many mornings I went through that drive-through and wrestled my Dr. Pepper and bean burrito while trying to drive because I was starving but wanted to avoid banging around the kitchen when I got home, which would have woken everyone up. Now I can barely stand the sight of Taco Bell, and I avoid eating there at all costs.

sleep

Studies show that driving while sleep deprived is actually more dangerous then driving while under the influence of alcohol. I have to agree with the scientists on this one. Your brain takes leave after so many hours without sleep – as if to say, hey, lady, your body may not be asleep but your brain is going to catch some shuteye one way or another!

During my cranky, sleep-deprived years when I was working around the clock, I know I did some pretty stupid things. One morning I was racing out the door to get to the office in time for a very important meeting. All the way to work I had the feeling I was forgetting something. At each stop light, I would check to see if I had all of the notes for my meeting. Everything seemed to be in order.

When I pulled into the parking lot at the office and opened my car door, I realized just what I had forgotten – my shoes! I had driven all the way to work barefoot and in my brain-fog hadn't noticed until I went to step out of my car. Now it was too late to run back home; the person I was meeting with would be arriving any minute. What was a gal to do? I decided to hurry and get in the conference room and have the receptionist show my appointment in when he arrived. I figured if I was already seated in the conference room, it would be much less likely he would notice my bare feet than if I walked into the room. This strategy seemed to work, or at least he didn't say anything about the fact that I was barefoot.

Once he left, I went in the back to our warehouse and found a pair of these goofy reflexology socks we were selling at the time and wore those around the office for the rest of the day. The next morning when I arrived at the office – with shoes on – I carried in a pair of flip-flops that remain in my desk drawer today. I highly recommend this! When your feet can't stand to have shoes on for another minute, just pull out your flip-flops and you will have an instant compromise! Your feet will be spared real shoes, and you'll be spared black feet. (What is it about office carpeting that turns your feet black?) For a gal who loves to be barefoot, that day I forgot my shoes turned out to be a blessing in disguise. It led to creating my beloved flip-flop drawer at work.

The Joys of Self-Employment

I have found that the irony is that most of the experiences we self-employed people endure are universal on some level. Just get with a group of us and you will see. We all share the trials, trauma, and triumphs of owning our own businesses. The joys are so plentiful that it is truly a wonder more folks don't join the self-inflicted suffering of the self-employed.

For years around the holidays I would sing, "All I want for Christmas is a *hat rack*." It seemed I was wearing so many hats that I didn't know which end was up anymore. At one point my name was in at least a dozen boxes on the org chart. I was working hours I frankly didn't think were humanly possible and getting grouchier by the minute.

I am not sure how (or why) my family put up with me for the first few years of the catalog. But my family kept on loving me even when, frankly, I was far from loveable. It wasn't that I wanted to work one hundred hours a week doing everything myself, I just couldn't afford to hire anyone else. At least that is what I thought. It turns out when you make enough costly mistakes – and you will when you try to do multiple jobs simultaneously – you will figure out that you can afford to hire somebody to help for less than it costs to fix your mistakes. Doing it all yourself for "free" can be expensive.

There are some things I did better than anyone else, and there were some things everyone else did better than I did. The trick is to figure out which those are and delegate. At some point, you can't afford *not* to hire on staff to help.

Being an Employer. Ugh.

Employees will be the biggest asset and the biggest pain in the asset every company will have. It's universal – it doesn't matter whether you own a sandwich shop, a construction company, a nanny service, an accounting firm, a retail store, or a *Fortune* 500 company. Whenever I get together with a group of business owners, it is the first topic to come up. We all struggle with the day-to-day managing of other people.

Oh, the tales I could tell. Okay, if you are going to drag it out of me, I will share just a few. We once went through four receptionists in a month. Hiring for our receptionist position seemed easy enough. We just needed somebody to answer the phone and do a little light clerical work. The first receptionist we hired seemed perfect until she started answering the phone "Femail Cremations" instead of Femail Creations. She just couldn't get it right *or* understand why it was such a big deal. I tried to explain the difference between a funeral home and a catalog, to no avail. The next gal we hired gave the impression we were running an entirely different kind of business. She answered the phone "Femails Creating" instead of Femail Creations. She was closer, but still way off the mark. Our third hire that month also ended in disaster when she thought the dress code didn't apply to her and the attendance policy was optional. We were still confident that the fourth time would be the charm. And it was – for a while.

For reasons still unknown to me, the receptionist position is one of the trickiest to fill. It is a key position in most companies, as the receptionist is the first person your clients will see and the first voice they will hear on the phone. You want to make a good impression. My husband and I share office space, and receptionists. Adding to the challenge, we also have different hours. It took us years to find a good solution. John DeGeorge, a business owner and friend in a similar situation, told us he finally split this position in two – one person works the first half of the day, the other person works the second half. This solved all of our problems. We no longer had to juggle everyone's schedule to cover the receptionist's lunch hour, we no longer had a gap in coverage between the two companies' hours, and most importantly we had back up. When one or the other couldn't come in or was late, the other could most often fill in for her. Two part-time employees can be more cost effective and efficient than one full-time employee, and dividing this job has also reduced the high turnover typical in this position.

In the spirit of "I did but you shouldn't," I must also say that hiring family and friends is a real challenge. As I interviewed other business owners for this book, I would ask what their biggest business mistake was, and I can't tell you how often they responded, "hiring family or friends." It can be wonderful, and it can also be awful. I have seen and experienced both of these extremes myself. Amy Peters said hiring a friend was the worst decision she made, Cindy Morgan said working with her best friend is the greatest part of her business. Either way, consider with caution. For me, the solution was telecommuting! I have found working with family is best when you're not all in the same physical space every day and you can't step on each other's toes.

Managing people was a very steep learning curve for me. I just assumed that because I am hard working and ethical, everyone else is, too. I also made the mistake of assuming that because titles and status meant nothing to me, they wouldn't be a big deal for anyone else. Wrong! Everyone feels appreciated in different ways. For some, that may mean just saying thank you and paying them well; for others, that is not nearly enough. Some employees are downright high maintenance.

In fact, I have discovered that knowing what motivates and makes your staff feel appreciated is the main ingredient to successful working relationships. The trick is figuring out what that is! Believe me, guessing wrong can be a costly mistake. I have given employees huge raises or bonuses in an effort to make them feel like valued members of the team, only to later learn that what they really wanted was more face time or to hang out together after work. I have given staff members unique opportunities that would help advance their careers, only to later learn what they really wanted was for me to compliment them on their new dress or say good morning with more enthusiasm. Sometimes it is an unreasonable – and frankly unthinkable – thing that a staff member feels they need to feel appreciated and stay motivated. It is not practical or prudent to be expected to be all things to your employees – boss, mentor, mother, and friend. However, discovering what your team members need to feel valued and trying to meet those professional (key word here *professional*) needs is the secret to having a happy and productive staff.

Creating the kind of company that treats our employees compassionately has always been important to me. I have certainly made my share of mistakes and often come up short as a boss due to lack of experience, but my heart has always been in the right place.

The fact is I deeply appreciate the work of each and every past and present staff member. However, this appreciation thing can be taken too far. I have jumped through hoops trying to make my staff happy. We have had everything from movie days to elaborate office parties, but that can create the old give-them-an-inch-and-they-want-a-mile problem. Sometimes the more you give, the more your employees want, and it is very hard to get that back into balance without seeming like an ogre.

The old cliché that the job expands to the number of hours a person is given to do that job is a cliché for a reason! It's true! Finding the right person for the right job is not always easy, but it is always important. Making the right match for each position in your company will maximize productivity and contentment.

From time to time, a person is just not the right fit for your company. When that is the case, either due to a mismatched skill set or a mismatched set of priorities, it is a disservice to both the staff member and the company to continue the working relationship. Sometimes letting them go is in their best interest.

Occasionally you will run across an employee who is just chronically unhappy or, even worse for business, who is addicted to crisis. If things are going too smoothly, they will just create a crisis to keep things stirred up. I have never understood the need for added stress, but some folks seem to thrive on it. Ultimately, you will realize that this is not *caused* by the job, but rather *is* a job – for a therapist, not for you or your company.

Over the years, many employees have come and gone as the catalog has grown and our needs have changed. Every business owner will attest to the fact that occasionally you will end up with disgruntled employees. That's all there is to it. Wish them well and move on. At the end of the day, they are the ones who will have to live with the knowledge they stole merchandise or company information, lied about their work, or participated in whatever behavior led to their no longer working with your company. Taking the high road is always the best approach. I always sincerely hope they find whatever happiness or peace they seem to be missing in their lives so they too can move on. I have had past employees so bitter and unprincipled that they have gone out of their way to spread lies about me or other staff members and gone out of their way to make sure we don't succeed. I frankly see that club of bitterness as a pathetic waste of time and energy. As Marian Anderson says, "As long as you keep a person down, some part of you has to be down there to hold him down, so it means you cannot soar as you otherwise might." So be the first one to move on and soar.

Because I take firing a staff member very seriously and don't let anyone go until I am sure it is my only option, I have never regretted doing so. I have, however, often said after they were gone that I wished I had done it sooner. I can't tell you how many times I made the mistake of keeping people around for far too long – even when I knew better. It is easy to become friendly with your staff and to like them too much to let them go, but trust me, you aren't doing yourself, your company, or your other employees any favors by delaying the inevitable. It sends a horrible message to the rest of the staff and turns a small problem into a big one.

When you know in your heart of hearts that an employee is going south, the best advice I can give you is to react quickly. Sometimes employees have expiration dates, and you want to make the necessary changes before they go sour and spoil the rest of the staff too.

Putting the Business in Good Hands

Speaking of firing . . . I think one of the most important steps an entrepreneur can ever take is firing herself. At some point, it is quite likely your company will outgrow you. If you are smart, you will recognize when this happens and act. Now, I am not suggesting that you must walk away and hand off your baby to somebody else, I am just suggesting that you send the baby to daycare. You will still be the mom, but you and the business will need breaks from each other, too.

A fellow catalog owner, Lucinda, was speaking once at a direct marketing conference when I heard her share advice that changed my entire perspective. She said that as owners we must always keep our focus on the future of our companies and that if we were still doing anything relating to the present – to today – we were mismanaging our time and energy. Our focus, she said, must always be on the future and the bigger picture.

At that point, all of my time was being spent on immediate issues. I was running around with my hair on fire trying to get the orders shipped out, resolve customer service issues, order inventory, pay bills, and manage the day-to-day operations of the catalog. Most of my time was being spent on the present and putting out that day's fires. The future of the business was always at the bottom of my to-do list instead of at the top.

Most entrepreneurs are great at starting businesses but not necessarily so great at running them. Those are two entirely different sets of skills. The issue I had with keeping people around for too long applied to me as well. I probably should have fired myself a year or two before I did. I best served the company by doing what I did best. In my case that meant the creative and merchandising side of the business and the bigger picture ideas and issues. Trying to run the day-to-day operations and manage the staff while traveling all over the country looking for new artists and creating five new catalogs a year just didn't make sense any longer, and I could see it was really becoming an obstacle for the growth of the company. So I fired myself and hired a manager, which allowed me to focus on what I was good at and more importantly the future rather than the present.

All of the employees now report to the manager rather than me. It was a difficult step to take, ironically harder on the staff than me. I had forgotten just how much everyone hates change. For the first few weeks, I thought we were going to have to break out the blankets and cookies and have story time while I read aloud to the staff *Who Moved My Cheese*, a great little book about change.

So, those are a few of my stories. I shared them here because I have found that other business owners and those about to start businesses are hungry for the truth. And the truth is that owning your own business can be deeply rewarding, but that dream also comes with some nightmares. Talking about those challenges and hearing you are not alone in facing them is refreshing.

Customers regularly tell me that it was reading about or hearing my story that led them to believe that they too could do it. When women hear, for instance, that I didn't have any catalog experience before I started Femail Creations, they are inspired to go ahead and dare to try something new, too.

Whether it's starting a business or living out loud in some other way, we have to conquer our fears and start somewhere, and hearing the stories of those who have gone before us can be a great catalyst to get out there and try something new.

manifesting miracles

13

We always attract into our lives whatever we think about most, believe in most strongly, expect on the deepest level, and imagine most vividly. — SHAKTI GAWAIN

WE ALL HAVE DAYS WHEN WE FEEL LIKE PULLING our hair out – the baby is crying, the phone is ringing, your sister wants to know why you haven't answered her email yet, your son forgot his lunch again, deadlines at work are piling up, there are more bills than money, and even Dr. Phil can't mediate the feud between your stepchildren! What is the secret to being positive despite all of that? Life is not one big long vacation, so how can we create that same kind of good vibe for ourselves every day? How do we manifest good things while feeling stressed? It's easy to feel good and stay upbeat while relaxing on vacation, but how do we maintain that same kind of energy when reality gets in the way?

Long before I knew what the words "affirmation" or "visualization" meant I was seeking to tap into my intuition and power to create. When I was in my early twenties,

I had a bulletin board on which I would hang up pictures, inspiring quotes, and images of things I hoped to one day have.

At the time, I had my heart set on a Volkswagen Jetta. So I went down to the dealership and test drove the model I was saving up to buy. I brought home a brochure and cut out the picture of "my Jetta" and hung it up on my board. I added images and torn pages from magazines, favorite quotes, snippets of this and a little of that, and over time it became my magical manifestation collage. Magical because I did indeed get that Jetta, and in fact, everything else on that board – which is truly amazing when you consider that for some reason I wanted a pink TV. At the time, I had never seen a pink TV, but I thought it would look so cute in my pink and gray bedroom – hey, this was in the 1980s. So I drew a picture of a pink TV and tacked that up on my board. Several months later I was shopping at a home store and froze in my steps when I saw a pastel pink TV! I still have that TV in storage, because I don't dare get rid of it – so powerful was that manifestation. (I think I just inspired *myself* to start another collage!)

There was something very powerful about collecting those images and looking at them each day. I had mine hanging in my bathroom – well, it is the one place you are sure to visit each day. Every time I brushed my teeth, there was my affirmation board looking back at me, reminding me to dream big!

I believe we attract to us that which we focus on the most. Of course, this same theory can work negatively as well. If we focus on the negative, we are likely to attract more of that into our lives. We all know somebody who constantly sees the downside in any situation and can't wait to share their bad news with you. Sometimes a bad mood can become a bad habit.

As the creative soul SARK said in her book *Succulent Wild Woman*:

> The negative can be so seductive. You can usually find someone to spend time being critical, judgmental, and dark with. Being positive does not mean being accepting of the negative, or ignorant of the issues, or the world situation, or anything else. It means seeing the grace in as much as you can see. Choosing succulence will enable us to be more alive, more contributing, flexible, and fresh.

It is my firm belief that we each have within us the power to manifest anything we deeply desire. Whether that is a new home, a new relationship, an incredible vacation, peace, a full bank account. But this isn't something you study for once and then you're done. Believing in the impossible and affirming our intentions is a never-ending process, and from time to time, we can forget that we have this power. It takes work, every day, to remain positive and focus on feeling the good things when stress is nipping at our heels. The trick to manifesting is to be open to receiving. Easier said than done, I know! However, I can tell you I have seen the rewards in my own life when I am indeed able to do just that.

Refuse to be closed off by worry, fear, and stress. Instead, stop, breathe, believe and open to receive.

stepping stone

One of my favorite ways to affirm my intentions is to wear jewelry with a meaningful word or phrase. Looking down at my wrist to see a bracelet reminding me to breathe or a reminder to simply be happy is a gentle way to bring us back to center. I also find a cheat sheet very helpful!

---

stepping stone

Make a list of things to feel good about. Next time you're stressed, grab that list and pick a happy topic to focus on. It'll get you through the rough patches. I guarantee it

---

I am also a firm believer that by clearing out our excess we make room for more abundance. As we let go of the old, we open the door to receive the new. Try giving away things with an abundant attitude and watch what happens!

---

stepping stone

Keep an abundance journal. End the day by writing down a few things you are grateful for.

Early on in the process of starting the catalog, I began keeping a miracle journal. It was just a simple blank book, but each time something magical happened I would jot it down. I was tickled to discover that the mere practice of writing these events down seemed to draw even more magic my way. When I finally found an artist I had really been searching for, I would make a note of that in my miracle journal. When I was honored to be awarded the Entrepreneur of the Year by the National Association of Women Business Owners, you can bet that went in my journal! When we found an incredible school for our son to attend, I couldn't wait to add that to my miracle journal. Whenever anything great personally or professionally happens that

I feel is a blessing, I jot it down in my miracle journal. It is a practice I highly recommend!

About the fifth year I was in business, I received an email from one of my customers. She was a Feng Shui consultant and offered her services to me – for free! She said she had worked with many corporations and small businesses to help them bring the principles of Feng Shui into their offices. I had been intrigued by Feng Shui for years and had read about huge corporations like Citibank and others who had hired Feng Shui experts to consult on building designs and space planning, but I had never really got the hang of it myself. My inability to read instructions got the better of me again. So when Alix contacted me to offer her services, I jumped at the chance to improve the peace and prosperity of Femail Creations.

When I told the staff that a Feng Shui expert was coming to our office, most of them said, "A Fung what?" I tried to explain, but ultimately gave up and told them all to just go with the flow.

I sent Alix a floor plan of our office with notes telling her what each room was used for. Alix divided the floor plan into nine sections, each one representing a different aspect: prosperity, fame, love, health, center, creativity, knowledge, career, and travel. This is known as the Bagua Map.

Alix drove six hours to get to our offices and arrived excited to get started. She must have known how badly we needed a boost to our prosperity zone! For most of the afternoon, Alix walked around the office spending time in each area, taking pictures, and making notes. Then she gathered everything up and said she would be back in the morning. She returned with a folder full of ideas!

It took Alix a while to get over the initial horror of what she had discovered. Apparently, our wealth, prosperity, fame, and recognition areas were the worst. No wonder we were still losing money! Once we reviewed how to improve those areas – and Alix strongly suggested we start there first – we went on to discuss how to improve all the other areas in our office.

It seemed paint was the 101 of Feng Shui, and we had our work cut out for us there since at the time our walls were all lifeless white. Alix also gave us great ideas about adding plants, fountains, crystals, and candles in specific places around the office to bring in more life. At our next staff meeting, I asked each member of our team to become "feng shui compliant" by adding a plant and candle to their desk and also by keeping their workspace very tidy. The truth is there were some eyes rolling in that meeting, but most loved the concept. One staff member was so into cheering us on with the whole Feng Shui adventure, we started calling her our Chi Leader.

The next phase required even more staff participation – it was time to paint. We started in our wealth and prosperity area since that was deemed to be a near crisis. Several of the staff members joined Jeff and me to paint our merchandising team's office an abundance-enhancing lavender and purple combination. We had a lot of fun doing it, and despite earlier doubts, in the end this color combo became everyone's favorite. We went on to paint most of the office – each workspace a different color depending on where it was located in the Bagua.

Years later when we moved to a new location, you better believe I got Alix on the phone to ask for her advice again. To this day whenever anyone new walks into our office, they always comment on how "good it feels" here. A nice compliment to Alix, the staff at Femail Creations, the kind of company I have worked hard to create, and the blessings of Feng Shui!

In the event your Feng Shui expert doesn't magically appear as mine did, I suggest starting with something as simple as a candle. It truly amazes me how much the effortless act of lighting a candle can change moods, energy, and luck. Lighting a candle remains one of the easiest ways I know to focus my intentions, shift my energy, or lighten my spirit. I have candles everywhere – on my desks, on my nightstand, on my bathroom counter (I light this one while I put on my makeup in the morning to start my day off right), in my kitchen, in my conference room at work, even in my suitcase so I can put one out as soon as I check into my hotel room.

Hanging poems and quotes or other inspiring cards can have a huge impact on your spirit. One of my favorite postcards is "The Real Woman Creed" written by Jan Phillips. I hang this where I can see it every day. Her words have been very healing for me, and I want to share them with you.

THE REAL WOMAN CREED

I believe that within me lies an extraordinary radiance, and I commit to letting my light loose in the world.

I believe that the source of my power and wisdom is in the center of my being, and I commit to acting from this place of strength.

I believe that I possess an abundance of passion and creative potential, and I commit to the expression of these gifts.

I believe that the time has come to let go of old notions and unhealthy attitudes, and I commit to re-examine what I have been told about beauty and dismiss what insults my soul.

I believe that negative thoughts and words compromise my well-being, and I commit to thinking and speaking positively about myself and others.

I believe that young women are in need of positive role models, and I commit to being an example of authenticity and self-love.

I believe in the relationship between my well-being and the well-being of the planet, and I commit to a life of mindfulness that regards all living things as holy and worthy of my love.

I believe it is my spiritual responsibility to care for my body with respect, kindness and compassion, I commit to balancing my life in such a way that my physical being is fully expressed and nurtured.

I believe that joy is an essential part of wellness, and I commit to removing obstacles to joy and creating a life that is full of exuberance.

I believe that a woman who loves herself is a powerful, passionate, attractive force, and I commit, from this day forward, to loving myself deeply and extravagantly.

oil for our lamps

14

To keep a lamp burning we have to keep
putting oil in it. — MOTHER TERESA

A S YOU KNOW BY NOW, I TRAVEL A GREAT DEAL ON business, and every time I do, I listen carefully as the flight attendants instruct us to put on our own oxygen masks before helping others. You won't do anyone any good if you have passed out from lack of oxygen. I think oxygen can be a metaphor for many things in life. If we don't meet our own needs, we will be less likely to be able to meet the needs of others as well. We may think we are doing them a favor by neglecting ourselves, but I am learning that is a bunch of bunk! We are doing everyone in our lives a disservice when we overlook our own needs.

Women are programmed to be all things to all people, at the expense of ourselves. Career consultant Amy Lindgren says:

Women run on expectations, the way a car is fueled by gas. And it doesn't matter whose: unspoken assignments from parents, bosses, clients, children, and lovers crowd our calendars' borders, in ink only we can see.

Women seem to have forgotten the *being* part of human being. We somehow bought into the human *doing* theory. This is an area I am still floundering in and have plenty of room for improvement and growth. Sometimes I think I am doing (no pun intended) so much better, and then I realize it has been over two months since I had a day off.

Treating ourselves humanely doesn't always come naturally. Take it from me. For years, I convinced myself that because the work I was doing was meaningful and because my mission was to help others, it was somehow okay to abuse myself in the process. I justified my long hours and self-neglect by focusing on empowering others. A big breakthrough came when I received a book on tape at the office for consideration to include in an upcoming issue of the catalog.

I often listen to tapes I need to review while driving to and from work. That night on the way home, I listened to Cheryl Richardson's book *Take Time for Your Life*. To say Cheryl's book changed my life would not be an overstatement. The fumes I had been running on were running out, and I was at a very dry place in my life. I learned that burnout can actually be a gift. After years of working extreme hours and neglecting even my most basic needs, I was beyond tired. My exhaustion ran so deep that rest alone couldn't cure it.

Cheryl reminded me that when your life feels like one long list of things to do, your true priorities – your most authentic aspirations and dreams for your future – get lost. Listening to Cheryl's tapes opened my eyes to just how off-track I had gotten and gave me a road map to help find my way back to myself.

I have found the thump to the head to be in direct proportion to our stubbornness to get our lesson. At first, the universe gives us a gentle little tap, but if we don't pay attention to that, the universe steps it up a notch and gives us a knock. When we still don't pay attention, the thump gets a little harder. Pretty soon, we have a genuine headache. If we still aren't paying attention, the thump gets serious. The more stubborn we are, the louder the message has to be. I confess I have been so stubborn at times that the universe all but had to take out a billboard for me to get the message.

I remember the first time I took a vacation after starting Femail Creations was when I went with my family to Lake Powell, where there are no phones, no cellular connections, and my email didn't work. It was downright liberating! Lake Powell is near the Grand Canyon and just as stunning. Spending a week under a ceiling of stars surrounded by walls of sheer red cliffs and a fluid carpet of deep green water was just the change of pace I needed.

One of the unexpected perks of this vacation was being able to completely relax about everything – including my appearance. There were no PR photo shoots to rush to and no business meetings to get presentable for. No makeup, hair dryer, or even clothing required, just a swimsuit would do. Heck, if I brushed my teeth in the morning I really thought I had gone all out! I was amazed at how freeing it was not to have to think about what I looked like. To simply shower, brush my hair, and be done – you know, as men get to do every day! Imagine having your complete bag of tricks consist of a comb!

I would never have guessed that the best part of the trip would be not having to "get ready" each day. How did we even get that phrase in our vocabulary? What are we getting ready for? How did we get sucked into all that fussing and painting and polishing? I want my money back!

I have a quote hanging up at home that says, "At worst a house unkept cannot be so distressing as a life unlived." Rose Macaulay already had that figured out back in 1881! I loved this notion so much I asked an artist to create a plaque just for the catalog with this quote on it. Admittedly, I am a gal who likes a clean house and I definitely function better in an organized environment. However, I don't know of anyone who was at the end of his or her life and wished they had spent more time vacuuming or dusting.

stepping stone

Clean the house less and live more!

Putting Oil in Your Lamp

Jeff and I were having dinner with friends one night when we began discussing how overwhelming being a new parent can be. My friend Lisa, the mother of a two-year-old and a newborn, said she felt like there was somebody hanging on her every second of the day, and she had long since given up on trying to find time for herself. Her husband and my dear friend Jay also agreed that Lisa was running on empty. I started telling Lisa my theory about putting oil in your lamp. I shared with her how long it took me to realize that if we don't take care of ourselves, we can't take care of anyone else. Lisa was in need of some serious oil!

We made a plan that night for the four of us to go to a Jimmy Buffet concert in a few weeks. I showed up with a beach ball and a batch of margaritas and a passion to show Lisa how to have fun again. Now whenever Lisa needs a break she gives us a shout and we head out for a refill. In fact just yesterday, I got an email from Jay simply saying, "Need Oil," and I knew exactly what he meant; it was time to play.

Oil for your lamp can come in many forms.

Take a moment for some quiet. Allowing yourself to sit down with a good book can be the ultimate luxury. My mother taught me that there is little a hot bath can't cure. When you can't afford to spare the time or money to go to a spa for the day, even carving out an hour for a pedicure can go a long way. Having my feet rubbed is my ticket to instant relaxation. Even during my beyond-busy years, I tried to squeeze in a pedicure every now and then, even if it meant dragging work along with me. It is amazing how good it can still feel to have your feet rubbed, even if you are looking at spreadsheets.

get together with friends

Getting together with friends is also a great way to fill up your cup. There is something so healing about belly laughs with the girls. My sisters and I all live in different states, but we try to plan a gathering at least once a year. Our last sister retreat was at my house. We had a three-day-long slumber party. We gathered in the kitchen on the first night. I made my black bean soup and jalapeño cheddar corn bread (just taking the time to cook felt like a luxury), and my sister Cynthia brought fresh herbs, so dinner was even more delicious. We ate until we were stuffed and laughed until we cried. My sister Jennifer taught us all how to play her favorite game, Cranium, and we enjoyed several hilarious rounds of that. Diane, the eldest of our sisters, is a massage therapist, and she treated us each to a soothing back rub. The weekend was just what we all needed – oil for our lamps.

exercise

For many women, exercise is salvation and their way of staying centered. Business owner and artist Gina Cerda told me she gets her endorphins five days a week in two Pilates classes and three dance classes. For me, exercise is something I often *think* about doing but rarely get around to. I do occasionally carve out a few minutes to get on the treadmill and crank up my Helen Reddy CD. "I am woman, hear me roar" has a way of getting a gal moving! But mostly I admit to being a yoga wannabe. In my mind, I do yoga, but that is about as far as I get. Before I started my own business, I used to take a yoga class three days a week and loved it! I take comfort in knowing that some day I will get back to doing that. For now, my exercise regimen mainly consists of what I can do at stoplights in my car.

cut yourself some slack

One of the best ways to keep oil in our lamps is to simply cut ourselves some slack. We put so much pressure on ourselves to be all things to all people – and to look great doing it. I am fortunate to often be asked to share my story in magazines, newspapers, and on television. When these public relation appearances began, I didn't know all the rules, so I didn't know I was breaking them. When the photographer showed up for my first professional picture, I was barefoot and wearing jeans. She looked a little puzzled and asked me if I planned to change my clothes. I explained that I was really a casual person and felt most comfortable without my shoes on. So we proceeded that way – with me in my jeans sans shoes sitting on the floor with my dog, Zoë.

Over time I realized that people expected me to be wearing a suit and looking more professional. I would stress about my hair, my makeup, what I wore, and every other detail you can imagine. When I was asked to be on the cover of a women's magazine, I felt enormous pressure to look right and make a good impression for Femail Creations.

The day of the photo shoot, I was having a really bad hair day. I had decided to wear my hair straight for this photo, and that turned out to be a mistake. My naturally curly hair is best blown straight by a professional. I can never do it as good as my stylist, Stephanie, can, and on that morning, I was trying to attempt it on my own. I didn't really like what I ended up wearing. And to top it all off, I was in pain – a lot of pain. I am prone to kidney stones, and unfortunately one of those jagged little suckers decided to act up that morning. So there I was, looking awful and feeling even worse. It was all I could do to literally grin and bear it through the hour-long photo shoot.

Months later when I saw that magazine, I cringed. I looked just about like I felt. It was one of the worst pictures of me ever – and it was on the cover. At first I was devastated, but over time that cover proved to be just what I needed. There was that awful photo of me on the cover, and you know what? The world didn't stop spinning, lightening didn't strike, nothing of any great consequence happened. It was just a bad, okay really bad, picture, but it wasn't the end of the world. It taught me to let go of the quest for perfection and anxiety surrounding photo shoots and PR appearances.

Several months later, I was in the midst of yet another photo shoot for a newspaper and again everything was going wrong. My curly hair has a mind of its own, and I never know when it is going to curl up and when it is going to just be wimpy waves. Needless to say, that day it really wasn't in the mood to get photo shoot ready. As usual, everything I owned seemed to be at the dry cleaner, so I ended up breaking the fundamental rule of photography and TV appearances – don't wear white. There I was with my bad hair and my white shirt and my smile. That is what I did. I sat down and smiled for the camera and then went on with my day. No significant damage done! It was a refreshing change from photo shoots gone by. I have learned to once again relax and break all the rules – even though I now know what they are!

Madeline Hemmings says, "With increased opportunity comes increased stress. The stress comes from multiple conflicting demands and very little in the way of role models." Amen! My favorite quick-fix for stress reduction is heading to the theater. A movie and a bucket of popcorn can cure even the most stressful day. My husband swears it's the only time my brain – which is usually going one hundred miles an hour – actually shuts off.

When I am in need of an oil change and don't even have time to take in a movie, there is nothing better than a few minutes with my Tivo. I have never really watched that much TV, just not my cup of tea; however the few shows I do want to watch always seem to come on when I am working late, so having a Tivo has changed my life! Now when I have a few minutes or *need* a few minutes, I click away and watch my favorite show, regardless what day it was actually on. A few minutes of *Oprah, Ellen,* or *The West Wing* and I'm back in action, with enough oil to get me through the next day.

keep your sense of adventure alive

Keeping our sense of adventure alive also keeps our cups full. If your spirit of adventure is buried so deep you haven't seen her in a while, it is time to let her out! One year while home for her holiday vacation, my daughter reminded me that "all work and no play" is no way to live. She insisted that I try something new. And she had just the perfect thing in mind . . . snowboarding. I found this to be far from perfect. In fact, I wasn't sure this was a good idea at all. But Harlie wasn't going to rest until she got her parents to go snowboarding; easy for her to say since she competes on a national level as a snowboarder.

Well, with a lot of trepidation and my daughter's gear on, I headed up the mountain. After a very short lesson in which Harlie felt she had covered "everything" we needed to know, she forced us onto the lift. Okay, that went well, but I couldn't imagine how I was going to get off! Sure enough, I fell every single time I tried to get off the lift, much to the embarrassment of those around me.

After a few runs up and down the bunny hill, I got the hang of thrusting myself to a vertical position (no small feat!) with this clumsy board strapped to my feet. The problem was I had no ability to stop, slow down, or steer. I had one speed and one speed only – fast. I was either horizontal trying to untangle myself after crashing into a tree, pole, or person, or I was vertical going ninety miles an hour careening down the mountain. There was no in between. I truly was a menace on the mountain that day. (To the nice woman on the skis that I plowed into and completely flattened, I apologize again.)

As sore as I was the next day, the truth was I was grateful to Harlie for giving me the shove (literally off the mountain) that I needed. It was fun to play again and connect with the spirit of adventure we sometimes forget we even have. Maybe "use it or lose it" applies here? Trying something new is another way we can nurture ourselves.

---

stepping stone

Take that painting class you have always wanted to sign up for, go backpacking for the first time, start the business you have been dreaming about, plant the garden you have always wanted. Dare to dream, dare to have fun!

The reality is that we are the only ones who can create time for ourselves and make self-care a priority. As writer Mary Wilson Little said, "There is no pleasure in having nothing to do; the fun is in having lots to do and not doing it." It is when we have the most to do that we most need to cut ourselves some slack.

the power of persistence

15

I find that every big success happens after I think I have exhausted 100 percent of my options. For me, success only happens after I give another 10 percent.

— BARBARA CORCORAN

NO MATTER HOW PASSIONATE YOU ARE ABOUT whatever it is you are doing, you will inevitably have times that you feel like you are in over your head. You will get tired, and you will feel like giving up. So when it happens don't be surprised; it is part of the journey.

On one particular day from hell, I was at the end of my metaphorical rope. I was up against a wall on a critical holiday catalog deadline while also trying to train a new staff member. I had checks to sign but no funds in the bank, a sick child at home, and a mountain of paperwork yet to face. I began by putting out the most urgent fire first and started proofing page after page of the catalog. After several hours, I had so many paper cuts I was starting to wonder if I was subconsciously trying to slit my wrists! When the receptionist walked into my office with a package, I was afraid to open it for fear it might be more work to pile onto my already deep stack.

As I bravely yet skeptically opened my mail, I discovered a gift from one of the artists in the catalog. Amy Peters had stayed up all night creating a special bracelet for me. It took my breath away. Moonstones alternated with sterling silver beads that each featured a design and special word of inspiration. The clasp of the bracelet was embellished with the tiny words "this is your year." Wearing that bracelet instilled me with hope and reminded me to keep the faith. Just knowing that somebody out there was trying to understand what I was going through and wanted me to know she cared made all the difference in the world and infused me with enough strength to get through that day and many hard ones yet to come.

Look, Mom, I'm on National TV!

Persistence is often about being willing to try anything to make your dream a reality. You know those goofy people who stand outside the *Today Show* with signs? Well, in a desperate attempt to get publicity, and somewhat on a dare by my sister Diane, I joined in with those early morning fools! And what a difference *Today* makes!

It all started when I headed to New York on business to attend a gift show. My sister Cynthia and my friend, artist Amy Peters, came with me. The three of us kept joking about getting up early and heading down to Rockefeller Center to surprise Katie and Matt. And for most of the trip it was just that – a joke! But on our last night in the big city we got to thinking . . . it would be pretty funny! So around 10:00 P.M. we started plotting and scheming to come up with some kind of poster. We headed down the block to an all-night drugstore and came up with some makeshift supplies. Then it was back to our hotel room to start creating our work of art for all America to see.

Our first attempt wasn't so pretty, but we kept trying. We couldn't actually find any poster board, so with female ingenuity, we took bright yellow folders and cut them apart and used duct tape to create something that resembled a long, skinny poster. With black magic markers, we painted our message for the morning TV viewers to see, in hopes that they would learn about Femail Creations over their morning coffee. By 3:00 A.M. we had a pretty good poster going – at least we thought so. Of course, it was also quite possible that delirium from lack of sleep had kicked in.

After a few hours of sleep, we hailed a cab and off we went. We wanted to be sure we were among the first ones there to insure a prime spot on the front row! Not many folks out and about at that hour. We took a picture under a digital clock outside Rockefeller Center just to prove we had arrived by 5:34 A.M. As the crowd gathered, Amy started the "take-one-and-pass-them-on" system to hand out Femail Creations catalogs to everyone there. We waited for our big moment to arrive and worked the crowd for support, even trying to bribe the cameramen to make sure we made it on TV. And since it was after all my sister Diane's big idea, we thought we should call her from our cellular phone and let her know it was time to fire up her VCR. We momentarily forgot (or at least we told her we did) that 7:00 A.M. in New York was 4:00 A.M. on the West Coast! What are sisters for, if not great ideas and an early-morning wake-up call?

Finally the moment arrived! Out came good ol' Al

Roker working the crowd. If only we had thought to borrow a baby, I am sure he would have come right over! We did get to meet makeup artist Bobbi Brown, since Amy bravely called her over as if she were a long lost friend. Thanks to Amy, Bobbi now has a copy of the catalog and a few of Amy's necklaces for her daughters. We didn't get to meet Katie because she was on vacation. But we did meet Matt and the lovely Anne.

I heard from several people who saw us on TV that morning. I even got an email from Matt Lauer's cousin, who said she loved the catalog and would put a bug in his ear about featuring it on the show. Our Web sales soared that day. In fact, we had so much fun and so much success that we decided to do this every summer.

The next year we dressed up in matching aprons that had been hand-painted by Laura, one of the artists in the catalog. Knowing Al loves to grill, we also brought along a big platter that said, "Al's Famous BBQ" and an apron for him too. Each year we tried to top ourselves. The next year we increased the size of our group, and we all dressed up like witches. Sure enough, Al couldn't resist finding out what these wild women were up to in August. The tradition lived on the following year, and we all dressed up in different-colored wigs with a sign that read "Femail Artists Wigging Out in New York City." That also got us on TV. Over the years, many advertising experts have contacted me to congratulate me on my guerilla marketing efforts.

Many years ago, I bought a plaque with the following Calvin Coolidge quote on it. It always does my heart good to read it again.

Nothing in the world can take the place of persistence. Talent will not; nothing is more common than unsuccessful men with talent. Genius will not; unrewarded genius is almost a proverb. Education will not; the world is full of educated derelicts. Persistence and determination alone are omnipotent.

it's never too late

16

The world is round, and the place which may
seem like the end may also be the beginning.

— IVY BAKER PRIEST

COMING FULL CIRCLE, I WANT TO END AT THE beginning. Many years ago a dear friend gave me a ceramic tile as a gift with this Nancy Thayer quote on it: "It is never too late in fiction or in life to revise." Seeing that quote each day was one of the things that planted my first seed of passion and inspired me to take the leap and start my own business. The sentiment of this quote still resonates with me now. I am not sure what the next chapter of my life will hold for me or how my dreams might evolve. But I do know I look forward to it with the same spirit of adventure.

Sometimes on the way to your dream you get lost and find a better one. It is okay to change our minds, and it's never too late to start. If you thought you always wanted to be a doctor only to discover after medical school that what you really wanted to do was open a bakery – open a bakery. Life is too short not to follow your heart. If you have always wanted to get your masters degree in sociology but think at age sixty it is too late, start anyway. In four years, you will be four years older, whether you got the degree or not. You might as well have the knowledge you've always wanted.

I have experienced many highs and just as many lows along the way. The hard work and challenges are overwhelming at times. During the trying times, the stress seems to seep into every cell of my body and soul. During the high points, anything seems possible. There were several times along the way that I felt like giving up and found myself questioning what I was really gaining besides lots of cellulite and debt. Going without sleep and facing chronic touch-and-go cash flow will cause any sane person to start to wonder aloud if it is all worth it. What I can tell you is YES! Creating meaningful work is worth it. Following our hearts, embracing our passion, and living our dreams is worth every bit of the courage it requires.

About three years into the business my doubts and the doubts of so many others were starting to take a toll. My confidence was starting to wane and my concerns were starting to rise. I was having a heart to heart talk with my husband about my fears when he asked me a simple question that put things into perspective in an instant. "Why did you start Femail Creations?" I quietly responded, "Because I wanted to make a difference." To which Jeff replied, "And you have. So no matter what happens in the future, Femail Creations will be a success. You set out to make a difference and you have – for so many women. You have inspired the customers who shop at Femail

Creations and offered a supportive venue for the artists who are in the catalog. You changed the paradigm about what shopping can mean. That is what you set out to do, and you have succeeded no matter what the accountants or your checking account says."

It was in that moment that I found the strength and courage to keep going for all the right reasons.

As I head into my eighth year of business, I am thrilled to share my happy ending with you. Femail Creations went public and I am now a millionaire – NOT! For some companies that will be the final chapter; for Femail Creations it isn't, and that may never happen. What I can tell you is that no matter what the final destination for Femail Creations, the journey has been worth it. I still have more courage than I have cash flow, and my sense of humor is still my saving grace. I am not laughing all the way to the bank, but I am still laughing. The mission of this catalog was to make a difference, and in that I feel blessed to have succeeded.

The amazing Gilda Radner once said:

I wanted a perfect ending. Now I've learned, the hard way, that some poems don't rhyme, and some stories don't have a clear beginning, middle, and end. Life is about not knowing, having to change, taking the moment and making the best of it without knowing what's going to happen next.

No matter what people say or how they try to get in your way, step out and state out loud: "I am taking my turn and following my passion."

 stepping stone

187

Find out who your most cherished inner self is and then embrace her wholeheartedly. Marilyn O. Sifford says, "You must create space in your life to enable your inner guide to share her wisdom, her creativity, her vision, her courage. Unleashed, she is the single most potent resource you have."

One of my favorite poems and sources of inspiration was written by the gifted Patricia Lynn Reilly. I wish for every woman to be blessed by these powerful words.

Imagine a Woman

Imagine a woman who believes it is right and good she is woman. A woman who honors her experience and tells her stories. Who refuses to carry the sins of others within her body and life.

Imagine a woman who believes she is good. A woman who trusts and respects herself. Who listens to her needs and desires, and meets them with tenderness and grace.

Imagine a woman who has acknowledged the past's influence on the present. A woman who has walked through her past. Who has healed into the present.

Imagine a woman who authors her own life. A woman who exerts, initiates, and moves on her own behalf. Who refuses to surrender except to her truest self and to her wisest voice.

Imagine a woman who names her own gods. A woman who imagines the divine in her image and likeness. Who designs her own spirituality and allows it to inform her daily life.

Imagine a woman in love with her own body. A woman
who believes her body is enough, just as it is. Who
celebrates her body and its rhythms and cycles as an
exquisite resource.

Imagine a woman who honors the face of the Goddess
in her changing face. A woman who celebrates the
accumulation of her years and her wisdom. Who
refuses to use precious energy disguising the
changes in her body and life.

Imagine a woman who values the women in her life.
A woman who sits in circles of women. Who is
reminded of the truth about herself when she
forgets.

Imagine yourself as this woman.

I encourage those of you who haven't discovered what
your passion might be to keep seeking and dig deeper
until you find it. For those of you who have found your
meaningful work, I applaud you. For those who have
found it and changed your mind, I say . . . it is never too
late to be what you might have been.

Take a deep breath and take the leap!

Dream Big,
Lisa

about the author

LISA HAMMOND IS THE FOUNDER OF FEMAIL CREATIONS, a mail-order catalog and Web site dedicated to celebrating the creative souls of women. Femail Creations was born out of Lisa's passion to empower women to dream bigger dreams.

Because of her unconventional nature, Lisa has become known as The Barefoot CEO. She writes a monthly online column for *www.femailcreations.com* called Girl Talk. Lisa was honored by the Small Business Administration as a Small Business Person of the Year in 2000 and by the National Association of Women Business Owners as an Entrepreneur of the Year in 2003. She currently resides in Nevada with her husband, their two children, and an Airedale named Zoë who doesn't know she is a dog.

For further information about this book or Femail Creations, Lisa can be reached by emailing *lisa@femailcreations.com* or by writing to her at PMB #131, 1000 North Green Valley Parkway #440, Henderson, NV 89074.

To request your own free copy of the Femail Creations catalog, visit *www.femailcreations.com* or call 800-996-9223.

to our readers

Conari Press, an imprint of Red Wheel/Weiser, publishes books on topics ranging from spirituality, personal growth and relationships, to women's issues, parenting, and social issues. Our mission is to publish quality books that will make a difference in people's lives – how we feel about ourselves and how we relate to one another. We value integrity, compassion, and receptivity, both in the books we publish and in the way we do business.

Our readers are our most important resource, and we value your input, suggestions, and ideas about what you would like to see published. Please feel free to contact us, to request our latest book catalog, or to be added to our mailing list.

Conari Press
An imprint of Red Wheel/Weiser, LLC
P.O. Box 612
York Beach, ME 03910-0612
www.conari.com